Dead Fish Don't Swim Upstream

Dead Fish Don't Swim Upstream

Real Life Lessons in Entrepreneurship

Jay J. Silverberg and Bruce E. McLean

BUSINESS EXPERT PRESS

Leader in applied, concise business books

First published in 2021 by
Business Expert Press, LLC
222 East 46th Street, New York, NY 10017
www.businessexpertpress.com

ISBN-13: 978-1-63742-157-4 (paperback)
ISBN-13: 978-1-63742-158-1 (e-book)

Business Expert Press Entrepreneurship and Small Business Management Collection

Collection ISSN: 1946-5653 (print)
Collection ISSN: 1946-5661 (electronic)

First edition: 2021

10 9 8 7 6 5 4 3 2 1

Democracy is the fundamental imperative that encourages and supports free enterprise. "Free" is the economic driver for free enterprise.

*Democracy creates the **umbrella** under which entrepreneurship thrives.*

Stifle democratic freedom, as we have seen overseas in thriving economic powerhouses such as Hong Kong, and investment capital flees, entrepreneurship becomes mired in politics and ideology and a once free spirit is no longer welcomed.

This book is dedicated to the Nathan Laws of this world, and to the freedom everywhere that nurtures entrepreneurship.

Description

Business academia offers an excellent entrepreneurial foundation. Then reality sets in. This book bridges the gap between academia and real business, to counsel by example, and to deliver timely, actionable recommendations to capitalize on opportunities, or to sidestep hidden business grenades. Advice is best delivered by those who have successfully walked the entrepreneurial trail, but not without incurring some scars along the way. That's us. For the university instructor or professor, this book adds another dimension to what is being taught, and facilitates the lecturers' ability to convey important business lessons in bite-size morsels.

Keywords

business; start-ups; minimum viable product; exit strategy; advisers; advisory board; deal making; entrepreneurs; sales; customers; boot strapping; funding; elastic ethics; investors; social responsibility; communications; partners; competitors; marketing; international deals; domestic markets; assets; soft assets; data rooms; business plans; markets; value propositions; revenue models; branding; promotion; business ethics; entrepreneurship; business strategies; business advice; success; dealing with challenges; academic business gap; business stories that teach; business life lessons

Contents

Prologue

Business is rarely straightforward. There are blips and unexpected but impactful events that will litter your pathway to entrepreneurial success. Many are exciting, but some are painful, or just hilarious. But, as with everything in life, there are valuable lessons to be learned.

All the stories recounted in here are real. We have lived them, both the good and the bad. So, here is an appetizer.

Meet Antoine.

Parade of the Muskrats

From the list of crazy events that have backfired hilariously, this one might take the prize. Let me tell you about Antoine, the factory maintenance guy.

The setting was a massive old brick building, built in 1871, and set over a stream that, in days gone by, powered the equipment inside through a series of massive leather belts and wooden cogs and wheels.

One can only imagine the discarded goodies tucked away in the damp basement over the last century plus. This was Antoine's base. He had his maintenance shop down there and, in his spare time, he hunted muskrats that wandered in from the stream below. For those not familiar with muskrats, think fat, fur-covered rats on steroids.

The pop of his rifle broke the office routine upstairs as everyone checked the office betting pool for the winners, based on Antoine's muskrat stalking below.

Antoine had a crush on Suzanne who worked in the office, and she teased him mercilessly. He was lovestruck.

As it happens, this factory was one of the 26 companies under my responsibilities as Group Comptroller/Troubleshooter. My role then was to sell this money-losing operation for its real estate or even heritage value. My likeliest buyer meeting was set up and we were prepared to launch our "dog and pony show" when bloodcurdling screams broke out in the adjoining main office.

It seems that Antoine, seeing Suzanne arrive in her new fur coat, harnessed up eight huge muskrats and was parading them on a leash throughout the office. His intentions were honorable. He told Suzanne that, in case her new muskrat fur coat developed any bald spots, he could furnish patches like the ones scrambling in eight different directions all around Suzanne's workstation.

The investors departed quickly, in utter horror (although I managed to later ease their concerns). Suzanne sold her muskrat fur coat now that she had seen what the fur donors looked like. And Antoine returned to the basement, confused, dejected, and still lovelorn.

And If I Were You...

1. Expect the unexpected. Controlling every part of a meeting or presentation is key. Normally, we all focus on the presentation content and comfort level of the attendees, but, as in the case of Antoine, you just never know.

2. Learn to laugh at the silliness that business, and life, might throw at you.

3. Practice the art of "skating" to try and salvage any situation that might turn ugly, or when faced with the unforeseen. Think of Antoine.

Introduction

Business academia offers an excellent entrepreneurial foundation. Then reality sets in. As the entrepreneur transitions into the real world, the pathway toward opportunities is littered with land mines. Advice is best delivered by those who have successfully walked the entrepreneurial trail but not without incurring some scars along the way. That's us.

The essence of this book is to bridge the gap between academia and real business, to counsel by example, and to deliver timely, actionable recommendations to capitalize on opportunities, or to sidestep hidden business grenades.

Business readiness for those tiptoeing into or immersed in entrepreneurship or management is key. With this book in hand, business students, the senior MBA or Executive MBA, or anyone interested in, or involved in business, will have instant access to counsel, steeped in decades of experience.

For the university instructor or professor, this book complements their curriculum with real-world perspective and examples. This adds another dimension to what is being taught and facilitates the lecturers' ability to convey important business lessons in bite-size morsels.

This book is reader-friendly, informative, and even entertaining, while delivering practical, realizable strategies and tactics to best address a host of business issues. Each chapter is divided into four sections:

1. *The Premise:* the specific challenge.
2. *Conventional Thinking:* how the challenge is normally viewed versus the authors' perspective.
3. *My Real-Life Story:* experiences that exemplify and clearly illustrate the topic at hand. Everybody seems to relate well to stories. This includes what lessons delivered here (e.g., "What did we learn here?")
4. *And If I Were You…* Actionable items offering a well-defined callout of realizable strategies that the reader can adopt and implement.

CHAPTER 1

Great Ideas Become Great Businesses

Be a Business Castle Builder

Premise

You need to define and embrace your own success. Are you an entrepreneur castle builder?

Conventional Thinking

While at Yale University, Fred Smith wrote a term paper on his idea for an overnight delivery service for small packages that could be delivered to all cities in the United States by air. He got a "C" grade on this paper. He went on to establish FedEx and changed the world.

Castle-builder entrepreneurs are focused, inspired, stubborn, and slightly rebellious. Not all go on to build billion-dollar empires, but most work tirelessly to build their dreams. They know what they want to do and mobilize all their resources to achieve whatever level of success they define as "having arrived."

Traditional business wisdom encourages entrepreneurs to follow a pathway, and, very correctly, lays out a process of steps to follow. However, what it does not stress is the absolute need for blind faith, for the audacity to try when others say "no you can't," the backbone to defy common sense or commonplace thinking, and the fearlessness to never stop trying to achieve what you alone define as your respectable level of success.

That might seem like a tall order, but baby steps can lead to giant leaps for those who do not lose sight of their bull's eye. Keep a "vision board," a visual collage of ideas and inspiration, and refer to it every day. It will help you stay on target and on vision.

So, what does success mean to you? It is a very personal question that only you can answer. Does business drive you? Do you consider business success as a milestone that defines your life, or do you use business merely as a tool to achieve a lifestyle choice?

When starting or growing your business, every cent you earn, or have invested, should go toward the activity that directly generates revenues. Most successful entrepreneurs spend less time shopping for leased luxury cars and more time protecting their intellectual property (IP) or strategizing how they are going to capture market share (or "steal" market share if the market is finite), or educate the marketplace about a groundbreaking product, service, or technology.

These companies started in the founders' garage or basement: Apple, Google, Mattel, HP, Amazon, Disney, Mag Lite, Microsoft, Yankee Candle, and Harley Davidson, to mention just a few. (In fact, this very book was created in our garage in the hopes of emulating 'the great ones'.)

Highly successful businesspeople will tell you that they work for personal satisfaction and "fun." But money has already bought them a level of contentment. Money has satiated them, but likely not you. Not yet, anyways. You should never lose that hunger until you reach or surpass your targeted level of achievement.

What are your parameters for defining success? Here are a few markers.

- *You have reached your goals (financial, personal, social hierarchy, recognition, etc.).*
- *You enjoy what you are doing, ranging from tolerance to loving it.*
- *You are maintaining a balance in your life between the things that are important to you.*
- *You feel mentally fulfilled.*
- *You have traded off what you were willing to let go of.*
- *You feel you have made a difference to people, to a cause, or to an industry; if that is within your goals.*
- *You have achieved happiness.*

My Real-Life Story

When I started my first business, I too was a basement-dweller entrepreneur. I had a haughty vision for success and a difficult pathway to displace some of my "ivory tower" competitors. The difference was they were gorged on past successes, and I was hungry to taste mine.

I designed and produced the most impressive website and promotional materials. I branded myself with a healthy dose of "elastic ethics," sounding like a player in the industry "old boys'" network.

I carried myself like a winner, while the lust for recognition gnawed within me. It was a case of playacting, and I was constantly on stage, which I relished.

I set my short-, medium-, and long-term milestones and fought to reach each one. There was more than one occasion when I needed to rethink and tweak my timeframes.

Eventually, I did "arrive" and developed a client portfolio of projects exceeding a billion dollars in capital projects. As I grew, I hired a great team, and opened offices in several large, metropolitan centers. I had finally earned the right to move my office from my dusty furnace room near my garage, into to a prestigious high-rise office tower—a setting designed to impress my high profile clients.

I had nothing left to prove, and my lifestyle, family, and other interests became my top priorities. Selling my company after a number of years of growth took care of that. I guess I had finally arrived.

And If I Were You...

1. Discover what success means to you and why it is important to you. This may take some soul-searching and inward-thinking, but it's worth the effort. And be honest with yourself.

2. Set out a series of milestones as to how you intend to succeed.

3. Identify the potential roadblocks that may defy your progress, and how you intend to mitigate these obstructions.

4. Catalog the resources you have at your disposal, including people who can help you. People can act as stepping stones to others, or multipliers who can refer business to you.

5. Generate an acceptable timeframe for your journey.

6. Be prepared to tweak and rethink things if you encounter hiccups along the way (and you will).

7. Above all, aim very high, but probably substratosphere. There is almost nothing worse than perpetually being just out of reach of your targets.

Taking the Business Leap

The Premise

If it's such a good idea, why isn't everyone doing it? Because they are not you.

Conventional Thinking

We are a nation of salary junkies. It's so true, and there is nothing wrong with it. Maslow's Hierarchy of Needs[1] has "physiological needs," including shelter and food and safety, encompassing employment and property. These are the most basic prerequisites for our survival. That basic paycheck is of utmost importance for our well-being.

Even for salespeople who work on commission, I don't think I have ever hired one who didn't want a base draw or salary, even willing to give up potential higher-level earnings for a steady sustenance income.

Then there's you, the entrepreneur. You create your own security, foregoing the biweekly pay for the opportunity to create a business entity that will generate excitement, fun, challenges, and, of course, greater remuneration than any job can deliver.

Focusing on the goal is a keynote characteristic of entrepreneurs. You need to be liberated, with few other pressing issues impeding your thought process, or monopolizing your time. That focus is sometimes interpreted as unemotional or uncaring when, in fact, it's just maintaining an unwavering focal point—your business.

Steve Jobs was a genius but often deemed unattached to anything but his work. When you think about how many years he spent doing something as "simple" as designing and redesigning the curve of the iPhone corners, you understand the dedication it takes to craft a successful venture.

This chapter is by no means about discouraging you from the entrepreneurial world. In fact, so much of the rest of this book supports those who are self-employed or go on to run successful businesses. But all

---

[1] "Abraham Maslow and the Pyramid that Beguiled Business." www.bbc.com/news/magazine-23902918

of that having been said, there are warnings you need to heed before you leap.

There are pitfalls, of course, including avoiding pseudo-opportunities ads like "Change Your Life Today. Road to Financial Freedom." If it's too good to be true, it probably is. Didn't your parents teach you that as it pertains to, well, everything?

There are also exceptions to this rule: opportunities that sound so good, and we convince ourselves there's no way they could be real, but they are. The rule of thumb here is that there are no steadfast rules, just good and bad business opportunities as defined by your own interests, needs, and confidence. Tread carefully.

You cannot accept thoughts as facts. Common sense dictates that you do your homework. Try to carry out your research without any blinders on. Carry out your due diligence, use third-party, impartial sounding boards and advisers, and then make your decision ever so slightly outside your comfort zone, but not too far afield. You still need to sleep at night.

Try to ignore opportunities that have short windows ("Contact us Today. Offers good for one week only"). Try to quantify promises made and ignore inflammatory claims and excessive motherhood, like "Join the most successful team in the world!" Being a risk-taker does not always imply being a lemming-like, blindfolded cliff jumper.

It is also worth briefly mentioning multilevel marketing (MLM) opportunities. Avoid them. They are packaged promises rarely kept. You know there are issues when your income is based on you buying inventory as opposed to actual sales, and when you are told (with no guarantees) that you will earn a lot of money in a very short timeframe. MLM is basically a job pushing someone else's products or services and continually lassoing friends and acquaintances to become reps. It's just another form of a job but with no salary.

Think twice (or more) before you sign any agreements such as a franchise, licensing, investment, or partnership deal. One mistake, a signature on the wrong dotted line, can change your life forever. There are a lot of smaller-scale Bernie Madoff clones in the business world.

Sometimes, you just need to consider divorcing yourself from a business or business idea gone rogue. Take time away and distance yourself so that your perspective becomes more objective. Quantify what went wrong, or is going wrong, and if it can be salvaged or remedied. If not, save the good bits, discard the rest, and find another more exciting endeavor to pursue.

So, if it's such a good idea, why isn't everyone doing it? Because few take the chance to go beyond their spheres of comfort. You do. Even fewer have the imagination to picture themselves at the helm of a living, breathing enterprise without dwelling far too long on the exhausting "what if it fails" cold feet/second-guessing syndrome.

Try stuff. Think beyond the sheep.

My Real-Life Story

In my younger and less prudent (interpret as "dumber") entrepreneurial days, and in my zest to capture that "golden goose" opportunity, I was tempted with the opportunity to virtually own the jade mining market on North America's west coast. I was dazzled by the numbers. I was secretive about sharing any tidbits of information, except with the small handful of investors I needed to bring to the table.

I did my due diligence with a sparkle in my eyes that betrayed my impartiality. I was a believer, but those beliefs were steeped in greed and misplaced trust.

At the very last moment, in fact, sitting in the lawyer's boardroom with most of the key deal participants present, I sensed an interplay among the attendees. Was it a smirk or smile passed between them, or an anxiousness to hurry and ink the deal?

I walked. It was painful, but I needed to listen to my gut feel and pay attention to the wise angel on my left shoulder berating the devil on my right. I was lucky. Two months later, the same players did cut a deal with a new party. It did not end well. I kept thinking how that could have been me.

And If I Were You...

1. Gage how important the salaried world is to your safety net. Assume you will have no decent income for six months. How will that impact you?

2. Treat every opportunity as a fresh start, with no preconceived notions. Then let your viability and impartial risk analysis, and selective input from others, help dictate your "go/no go" decision.

3. For any business idea you may have, or one that is being offered to you, there is a very strong likelihood that someone has tried it, or is in that business now. Role model. Deep research will uncover a host of good as well as telling facts.

4. Question everything. Don't take anything at face value. Do not indulge in third-hand, broken telephone input. Information tends to get distorted as it passes from person to person.

5. Despite your best intentions, chances are you are not in this alone. There are partners and family to consider. Anyone who will be directly impacted should be part of the decision-making process.

6. My goals in business have always been "fun and money." What are yours? Etch them in your mind.

Let's Start Here. Are You Entrepreneurial Material?

The Premise

What makes an entrepreneur tick? Hard work and drive alone don't even come close.

Conventional Thinking

We all know the time-honored attributes associated with entrepreneurship, and, for the most part, they are true. But in compiling a shopping list of characteristics exhibited by genuine, hardcore, incurable entrepreneurs, the traits generally bantered about are hopelessly incomplete.

If you have "walked the walk," you may recognize bits of yourself here. However, and most importantly, for those thinking of going into business, or those doing a periodic self-evaluation of what they bring to the table in terms of their entrepreneurial skillsets, those highlighted in the following chart are the critical components of the passionate business devotee. Certainly, nobody teaches you this stuff. You have to live it.

This is not a scorecard, or a test. Very few businesspeople exhibit all of these virtues. Perfection is way overrated. But, as you tiptoe through the list below, you will undoubtedly recognize where you do perform well and also what gaps in your business makeup may require some shoring up.

Feature	The Bona Fide Entrepreneur
Thick skinned	There will certainly be occasions where you will be ridiculed, or be the object of jealous competitors' derision. That is a price that aggressive entrepreneurs pay. You ignore it. In fact, you thrive on it since the more people talk about you, the more they fear your ascendance in the marketplace.
Deflecting rejection	You are not failure-adverse. In fact, you see failure as a part of a learning experience. You have no love of failure, just an acceptance of same, and more so than others.
Set rules	Others' rules are not for you. Setting your own rules is part of your modus operandi. You live your business life by the standards you set, and your very own rules, shaped to help you meet your objectives. Preconceived expectation standards are stifling to you.
Be a user	You have no hesitation in using people as stepping stones, or as multipliers to connect you with others. This is nothing personal. It is strictly a way to get what you want, and although it may carry certain social stigmas, there is no guilt associated with any of this for you.
Leap of faith and unshakable belief	You tend to lead with your gut feel. That's not to say you do not believe in research and planning, but decisions are often made because you simply know and believe it is the right thing to do.
Hidden vulnerability and secure with insecurity	You may very well be a child at heart, or have certain fears and apprehensions, but they are yours alone, not to be broadcast or shared. You have invisible insecurities.
Pretense of invincibility	Real or perceived, you are invincible, and bulletproof. You may well believe in destiny choosing and guiding you.
Renegade	Leaders are perceived as renegades, and you enjoy playing the part. It becomes part of your persona. You can act outrageous, but within limits so as not to be perceived as outlandish.
Clairvoyance	Crystal-balling is a characteristic attributed to you, but more so when you are successful. You are a visionary when you succeed, and a resilient player when you bounce back from missteps.
Skittish	Despite your dedication to carrying out your gameplan, you tend to jump at any deviation or sidestep. It is a survival skill that allows you to take rapid corrective action, or act on an opportunity quickly.
Playful	Humor and self-deprecation seem to be part of the true entrepreneur's public personality. It shows others that you too are human. However, it is just an act that you have perfected.

Feature	The Bona Fide Entrepreneur
Self-worth	You are comfortable with who you are and what you can achieve. In fact, your self-worth is cast in stone and is never questioned. You have leaped beyond the first several basic needs tiers of Maslow's Hierarchy of Needs and moved upward toward deriving satisfaction by working to succeed.
Roleplay	Theatrics may be an important component of how you create and maintain your public image. You chose the business rebel character more often than not.
Unachievable standards	By setting haughty business goals, you are constantly striving and reaching upward. Even if your goals are unattainable, the skyward process still drives you.
Feast or famine	You are accustomed to periods of celebration and times of financial deprivation. That is one of the most difficult realities of being reliant on yourself for financial sustenance.
Live the brand	There is little separation between you and your company. You live the role.
Never disconnect	Regardless of where you are, be it during a family vacation, or dinner out with friends, you cannot let go. You will read e-mails and take calls and be available.
Driven by the heart	65% or more of entrepreneurs are driven by passion. Money is important, but not as key as an almost fanatical zeal to succeed because, in your heart, you must.
Anally retentive	You execute a process, step by step, in a determined progression that belies any fear of failure.
Pliable	You have the ability to accept and roll with change as long as it does not interfere with your end goals. These are immovable.
Chameleon qualities	You are infinitely adaptable to any situation. You can roll up your sleeves and swear with the best of them, or maintain the snobbish decorum of the elevated. You can become whomever the scenario calls for.
Excellent communicator	You likely have the "gift of gab," can join and dominate any group discussion on any topic. You are the master of small talk. You are a great salesperson because you are such a strong believer in what you are promoting, that is yourself.
Image is everything	How people perceive you, or, better stated, how you let people perceive you, is so very important. You have a public image that needs to be consistently you.
A pension fund	You're it. You recognize that you are your own safety net. You make provisions for your downstream financial needs.
Business ethics	Finally, where would we be without an observation of your business ethics? They are flexible. You bend the rules, but never fracture them. You often walk along the edge between what you can do and what you shouldn't.

So, be totally honest, how does your character and temperament fit the entrepreneur mold?

My Real-Life Story

I have had the opportunity to design, found, and spearhead a number of successful businesses. With each and every one, I had a carefully designed gameplan that detailed milestones that needed to be achieved. These were, in fact, a series of baby steps, and the realization of each, motivated me onward.

I set goals that I knew were ridiculously high. But it gave me and my team something to shoot for. In several instances, we actually met those goals. What did I do? I set new, even higher goals.

Speaking of people, I always hired those who I felt could adapt to my style and adopt my aggressive expectations. People with no baggage.

In the early stages of my ventures, I playacted the role of a confident and successful businessperson, even though I was neither. I needed to exude this make-believe image to build a client base as well as a loyal team proud to be associated with the companies.

My marketing and promotional campaigns tended to border on the slightly outrageous, with guerilla marketing as my favorite tactic. I needed to make noise, which I did. Loudly.

I sought out speaking engagements at various levels, from Chambers of Commerce to trade shows and large-scale conferences. On all occasions, I was the consummate, uncompromising entrepreneur in how I carried and presented myself.

I never really let it go to my head. I realized that the persona was key, but, in the grand scheme, it was playacting in an ivory tower residence.

In the end, my entrepreneurial model was successful. I honed it to what worked. In fact, it became part of me, my demeanor, my work ethics, and my incessant drive. It still is a big part of my business-schizophrenic character.

And If I Were You...

1. The chart encompasses many of the winning features of successful entrepreneurs. Carry out an assessment, based on the previous chart,

and identify if and how you exhibit the makings of the "bona fide" entrepreneur.

2. Have others, preferably your close associates, assess you as well using the same standards.

3. Where there are identified gaps, pay attention to what these shortcomings might be, and how they impact your business. Fix them. Plug the holes.

4. Never let your guard down in public.

5. Watch what feedback you get from others around you, your clients, and your marketplace. They are your mirror.

6. Many of the features highlighted in the chart, if not part of your current makeup, may be acquired through practice and role modeling, and diligent adherence to the kind of entrepreneur you want to be.

7. Design and live your entrepreneur identity, personally, and through your company.

Please, Please Take Off Those Rose-Colored Glasses

The Premise

Business change is inevitable. Eyes open, head up.

Conventional Thinking

In any business environment, the entrepreneur, CEO, or manager has any number of tools with which to safeguard and grow their business. The one certainty is that things change. Market and currency fluctuations, trade wars, and technology's dizzying pace can have huge and sudden impact on your business. Add to that pandemics, politics, and international strife, all threats over which you are powerless, and it is clear that guiding your business through squalls and storms requires crystal-balling.

When the economy is strong, your main concerns are maintaining the status quo of your firm's products or services, keeping up with demand, or leapfrogging your competition. Looking and planning ahead is a straightforward and regimented exercise. I still see many businesses, with blinders on, planning their future based on hindsight, historical market trends, and an antiquated belief that if I have succeeded up until now, I will continue to do so.

Trust me. Dead fish don't swim upstream.

Often it is a flawed arrogance and a "we are invincible" mindset that create dead fish. Here are just a few floaters.

- *"Television won't be able to hold any market it captures."*
  "People will soon get tired of staring at a box every night."
  —Daryl Zanuck, 20th Century Fox, 1946
- *"There is practically no chance communications space satellites will be used to provide better telephone, telegraph, television or radio services."—Arthur Sommerfield, US Postmaster General, 1961*
- *"Remote shopping, while entirely feasible, will flop."*
  —Time Magazine, 1966
- *In 2000, Blockbuster Video rejected the idea of streaming movies and turned down an offer to acquire fledgling Netflix for $50 million. Instead, they launched their own competing by-mail subscription DVD service. Blockbuster filed for bankruptcy and closed all of its stores in 2013. Netflix's net worth as at April 2020 was $125 billion.*
- *"There's no chance that the iPhone is going to get any significant market share."—Steve Ballmer, Microsoft CEO, 2007*

Insight and critical thinking are skills that all businesspeople need to hone. And to that end, the need for future-forward predictions has become so critical, not only for your existing business, but to be at the forefront of new opportunities as they arise, or are about to. Thinking several years ahead, ask yourself the following.

- *Where is the economy itself heading, and how will it impact my sector of business?*
- *Which of my competitors has grown dramatically? Failed dramatically? What can I learn from these?*

- *Assuming technology is the fastest growing component of our world, how is it impacting our customers? Our products or services? How can we adapt?*
- *Will what I am doing still be relevant in several years, or does my company have a "best before" date?*
- *What influences or influencers may dramatically impact the stability of my marketplace? How can I adapt, fall into place, or help lead the charge?*

My Real-Life Story

My client was in the technology entertainment business, meaning they developed a system for hotel pay-per-view movies. The system included retrofitting hotels and motels to accommodate movie delivery, and that, in itself, represented a host of proprietary in-room gadgets and systems like movie selection boxes, integrated hotel services and menus, advertising, and front desk billing software.

My role was to develop an investor package, which included due diligence into the company's viability, the kind of questions investors would ask.

There were a number of issues that my trends analysis revealed. Netflix was ramping up its streaming services. iTunes and Google on-demand movie rentals were gaining popularity while laptop computers were becoming faster and sporting higher definition screens. This made entertainment very portable, even in hotel rooms.

My client's best before date was not long off. All the signs were stacked against them. I could see that they were being leapfrogged.

As well, I concluded that my client had entered this market as an "also-ran." A major competitor had a stranglehold on the major hotel chains, and my client was having difficulty signing distribution rights for the in-room movies themselves.

I did not sugarcoat my results and suggested most emphatically that they identify other applications for their technology and hardware package where their solutions represented a degree of leading edge with somewhat greater life expectancy. It took some convincing to wrench them out of their trance, but, thank goodness, they did and they are still thriving.

And If I Were You...

1. Stay informed, alert, and nimble.
2. Designate someone as a "VP Change," with their job description to monitor markets, trends, competition, including upcoming changes destined to arrive in the marketplace. Have your VP Change work with a dedicated, and likely introverted researcher who thrives on following market and industry changes that can impact on your business. Meet regularly with them and listen.
3. Never wear blinders in crystal-balling your business and your sector. Color blindness can be fatal.
4. Change, both from within and from without, is inevitable. Your reaction to it, with sufficient notice, should be a process, and not a knee-jerk reaction.
5. Understand that the business you have today may very well not be the business you are in tomorrow.

CHAPTER 2

Business Planning, Startup Research, and Feasibility

Your Business Plan Is Living, Breathing, and Everchanging

The Premise

Your business plan is more than a one-off document. Your business plan is you. It speaks of you, about you, and for you. It can help you manage the development and growth of your business and shape how outsiders see you.

Conventional Thinking

Conventional opinion is that a business plan is created so that everybody can understand what you are doing and how you are going to do it. That is a very broad-based definition. The truth is that a plan must play to an audience and must be specifically tailored to elicit a reaction from within your company and management team, or from outside parties such as investors, bankers, and potential strategic partners.

In fact, your plan is your guidebook that you use as the road map toward the growth of your company, or your opening bid in negotiations with parties whom you want to bring into your fold.

Your "business plan" is best described as your just one of your stable of "business plans." There will likely be several. Each plan needs to be specifically designed to appeal to an intended audience or morph into a Cinderella coach going to the ball to impress others. Your business plan is a chameleon.

Business plans serve both internal and external needs. Business plans can be your best friend. It's all about how you are going to use them. You need to ask yourself, "Who is the audience for my business plan?" That is a critical consideration.

- ***Internal: A plan for you to follow.*** *It needs to be realistic, grounded, and responsive. It demands that you scrutinize what is important in your business and generate a plan that defines what actions you need to take to realize the growth you are anticipating. In short, it needs to look at what you have, what you need, and how you will get there.*

- ***External: A plan for funders, investors, or partners.*** *An external plan needs to respond to what money players need to hear, in a language they can quickly grasp and in the brief attention span investors allot to reviewing opportunities.*

The Internal Business Plan	The External Business Plan
• Internally, the plan should be a compilation of the commitment of the core group that developed it.	• Externally, it can represent your company's plan to investors, banks, or outside stakeholders.
• The real value of your business plan lies in actually defining a road map on how you are going to manage and grow your business.	• Your business plan creates credibility with your stakeholders, and it speaks to the key questions of how you are going to make money, when, and how much.
• A good business plan is built from the ground up. Think of children playing with building blocks; you put the first ones on the floor and then start to stack them up. It's a combination of your business concept and a ton of external research that validates your business premise.	• Most good business plans can be summarized into a 10-page document that includes earnings graphs, your business model, and research reports that support your business concept. This is what many outsiders will quite literally base their analysis of your business on.
• Your business will evolve as it grows, and your business plan should be continually upgraded to reflect this growth and the changes that you embrace.	• The problem with most 300-page business plans is that nobody outside your company is going to read them.
• Remember that a good business plan is a living and evolving document. Don't just bury it in a dusty filing cabinet after it has served its initial use.	• This is where you need something that is more than just the executive summary that precedes most business plans. You need a *"business plan for dummies"* specifically for outsiders who want to understand your company, and they want to do it quickly.

The Internal Business Plan	The External Business Plan
• For the most part, internal business plans are poor at telling the company's story to outside audiences. It's a detailed, slightly boring planning document. • Your business plan is your bible. Own it and use it.	• One of the things that everyone wants to know is your "aha" moment—the one that launched you on this course.

My Real-Life Story

One of my ventures had to do with a never-tried-before advertising medium for taxis and limos. We had the technology, but what we needed was a beta test in a large metropolitan area. We arranged to do a presentation to a major city's taxi commission that represents thousands of cabs. It was a "David versus Goliath" moment.

Before going to the meeting, I researched the proposed attendees, the commission, and the board members. They were all hard working, basically blue-collar types who had worked their way up through the rank and file. With this information in hand, I had our people do a model-size mock-up taxi that had our advertising medium built in.

My business partner, who was to present with me, had created an awesome presentation. It was about three inches thick and weighed a couple of pounds. It was very impressive when it was thumped down on a boardroom table. We demonstrated that we had done our homework. But this plan was not really designed for this group. There was a communication problem.

As the group was getting restless, I stepped in with my remote-control model taxi and took it for a spin around the entire boardroom, leaving enough time for each of the 20-person board to get a good look at what we were proposing.

It was virtually a done deal. My partner then delivered the PowerPoint to a much more receptive audience, capping off a successful meeting. We got our beta test connected to a highly recognized big city organization. We were on our way.

The combination of a business plan to impress, a PowerPoint to explain, and a highly creative (and risky) maneuver with a mock-up model of their taxis with our novel advertising delivery package, is what it took.

The lesson here is to get creative. Use all the tools at your disposal. Build on your business plan and go a little crazy when you know the intended audience will appreciate the edgy gesture.

And If I Were You...

The Internal Business Plan

1. For internal planning purposes, understand that when you are creating a business plan, you are building a road map for your business that will primarily be used by you and your core management group.
2. Break your plan down into various management agendas (sales, operations, and IT) that can be reviewed each week to assess your progress. It will keep you on track.
3. Continually revise your plan to reflect management input, new timelines and the multitude of changes that you will encounter as your company evolves.
4. Don't assume the business plan you create today will still be viable tomorrow. Things change. Technology leapfrogs. Competition crops up. Stay alert.

The External Business Plan

1. Understand that the goal of external business plans is to generate a positive reaction and a ratifying response.
2. Focus on the sell and the potential and go easy on the 25 pages of "risk analysis."
3. Know your audience before you structure a plan that will push their "hot buttons," that are their areas of interest.
4. Restrict access to financials and other "secret sauce" via web access.
5. Create 4-, 10-, or 20-page business summaries that make it easy for people outside your company to understand your story. These are often called "ticklers" and their goal is well-defined by their name.
6. You can and should restrict access to information on patents, company's confidential information, and IT material from within the general body of your business plan. This info can be summarized

and only disclosed via a secured website and only when you deem it necessary.

Start at the End Before You Begin

The Premise

Figure out what you want out of your business adventure before you even launch.

Conventional Thinking

I am pretty sure you have been told, or taught, that a business idea needs to be well researched, thought out, and meticulously planned as a precursor to being shared. Reduce the risk, make fewer mistakes, and stay on course. That's conventional wisdom.

While all of this is relatively sound advice, there is one aspect of business that, sadly, seems to take a back seat, namely, your dream. Entrepreneurship is a highly emotional decision.

You have gone into business for a reason, and part of that is your vision as to how far you want to take this adventure and what you want out of it all when you arrive at your journey's end. Never ever lose sight of that destination.

Launching your enterprise is simply a first step. Succeeding along the way is just your odyssey, and you are not there yet. However, fulfilling your business dream, the goal that you clearly defined before you started your business, is your true destination.

That destination could well be what drove you into embarking on your voyage in the first place. But, until that milestone is reached, you are simply en route. So, start at the end before you begin.

It is also far easier for you to "think big" right from the onset, even if you are starting small. Setting the bar higher than your comfort level early on is a great way to continually reach new heights for your business.

Right from the onset, here is what you should consider doing.

1. *Set measurable objectives (numbers to achieve, markets to penetrate).*
2. *Set qualitative goals; what you personally want out of your business journey.*

3. *Keep motherhood locked away. Your goals should be specific, nothing vague.*
4. *Share your goals with people close to you. This will make them more real, and you are certain to be reminded of them if others see you stray.*
5. *Set milestones and timelines that are attainable, but not easy to achieve.*
6. *Identify potential roadblocks and develop strategies to climb over them.*
7. *Continuously remind yourself of your destination and the joys of arriving there.*

It is also far easier to dream, scheme, and set your targets while you are fresh, and before you have been inundated with the reality of day-to-day business challenges. A little naivety and startup junkie enthusiasm help the process too.

My Real-Life Story

Story #1

In several of my businesses, I initiated strategic planning sessions with my team. Usually held at a resort getaway, we plotted the future of the company, ensconced away from distraction. We developed formidable plans for world domination and achieved "buy in" from most participants, all of whom were encouraged to present their ideas.

When we returned to the office, confident that our plans were practical and realizable, we were immediately thrown back into the reality of business at hand and the pressures that were awaiting us. That is not to say that our creative strategic planning was a waste of time. Far from it. We implemented some of the ideas. However, the master plan, the destination of my goals, was often buried in the scrum of business.

Having said that, there was one occasion where my end objective was crystal clear. It was scribbled on a napkin while sitting with friends in a greasy spoon restaurant. It was a launching pad for one of my more successful endeavors.

And for the entire life span of that particular business, I actually had that ratty, oily napkin framed over my desk as a reminder of my destination. It worked.

Story #2

I provided strategic planning and advice to all manner of companies, from startups to multinationals. However, in regards to early-stage goal setting, there is one story that comes to mind.

This one health care technology company was based on true scientific genius. They had developed a new heart stent, and I spent close to an hour listening to how great it was (and it was) and how smart they were (great credentials). In fact, they were so wrapped up in themselves and their new adventure in entrepreneurship that I actually had to stop their self-aggrandizing presentation to ask them to focus on what they were actually developing.

When I inquired as to what they wanted out of their business experience, they fell quiet. They had not looked beyond their technology and the science behind their invention. No one had a clue that there was a life downstream beyond their company. It was a classic case of entrepreneurial exuberance overshadowing their big picture destination dreaming.

And If I Were You ...

1. Develop an "end of the day" checklist of what you want to achieve, professionally, and personally.
2. Create a road map gameplan to take you from today onward.
3. Don't stray. Focus on your destination. Don't get distracted by other opportunities or side hustles.
4. Keep track of how you are travelling along. I used to literally create a map of my trip and destination, and mark off my "mileage" every couple of weeks when I revisited it.
5. Try to define and understand why you are going into business, or have gone into business. Your motives will help determine your end goals.

CHAPTER 3

Launching a Business Like You Really Mean It

No-Nonsense Tough Questions for the Startup Entrepreneur

The Premise

Starting a business? There are some tough questions to ask yourself. Some answers can be motivating, while others can be very personal and unabashedly embarrassing. Regardless, pay attention to the responses, whether they are what you wanted to hear, or not.

Conventional Thinking

Launching a business is an exciting event. It is highly charged and quite often life-changing. It all starts with an idea, or an opportunity that presents itself to you, and, traditionally, launches an exploratory process of market and competition research, "what if" numbers crunching, business plan game planning, and a mind-numbing buzz that encapsulates the passion of your proposed journey.

Passion is an apt description. It is essential in business. Without intensity and zeal, your venture is likely destined for the ho-hum doldrums that befall the mountains of commonplace, also-rans and, in many instances, the stockpile of business failures.

A critical component of your business planning, long before you arrive at your "go/no go" decision is a list of tough questions you need to take time to think about before you answer honestly. You need to be truthful to only one person—yourself.

I am humbled and apologetic to state that this line of questioning can only be generated by those who have occasionally messed up, leaped haphazardly at the shiny coin on the road, or made business decisions without taking off those rose-colored glasses. I am guilty, but I have learned from my missteps and moved on. I can, however, pass along some gems for your unfeigned scrutiny and deliberation.

The nature of these probing and delving scenarios is more like being subjected to a third-degree self-examination, and outside the boundaries of textbooks and provisional business thinking. Hand-in-hand with the more traditional process and stages of academic-taught business planning, the following questioning better prepares you for the taxing rigors of entrepreneurship.

1. *Why are you doing this?* There are right reasons, like a sincere desire or confidence in your proposed endeavors, and an even greater array of misguided logic like greed, revenge, or simply a dislike for what career decision you find yourself in. Then, there are the illogical motives like "this looks easy", or "others do it, why not me?" or "I can get rich pretty quickly." None of the latter qualify you to start a business. Move on.

2. *Does the opportunity fit you?* I am not talking about skillsets and experience. Those are separate issues. Important, yes, but different than "fit." Do you have the staying power to overcome certain roadblocks that you will encounter? Are you comfortable with risk-taking? Capable of impartial decision making? Agile enough to change direction mid-stream?

3. *Comfortable with transition?* Have you thought about moving from a paycheck to a self-driven income? Can you comfortably live with the insecurity particularly inherent in the formidable stages of business startups? You are not alone in this journey. Do you have the unwavering support of your partner and family? That is also critical. You cannot succeed if you have resistance from within your ranks.

4. *Are you ready to sacrifice?* This sounds ominous, but, in reality, entrepreneurship commands your time, focus, and the predominance of your everyday thoughts. Beyond that, business startups draw on your financial resources. Personal capital is likely a major contributor

toward the funding of your business. Will this be an issue? If the ramp up period is longer than you had anticipated, can your finances carry the expenses of your venture's burn rate cash flow?

5. *You have an image of "success." Will your business deliver success to you?* You have set certain goals and business aspirations. You have expectations. You know where you want to be in "*x*" years. You have additional ambitions in terms of social status, community and family standing, and position. Do you see this business providing all of that?

6. *Failure is not an option. Or is it?* Most businesses stumble, particularly in their launch or early stages. There are always roadblocks to circumvent, new pathways to discover and pursue. Your final business is often different from your original enterprise model. How malleable and adaptable are you?

These are all critical questions for you to consider and to get comfortable with. While the list is by no means all-inclusive, it does represent an important cross-section of drivers that can make or break a business—your business. It's best to deal with these issues in your company's infancy.

My Real-Life Story

We proudly share stories of our successes but often downplay our failures. That is human nature. However, experienced entrepreneurs gain important perspectives from falling short of success, or experiencing temporary setbacks.

I was young, impressionable, and most eager to transition from employment to entrepreneurship. Perhaps too eager.

An opportunity was presented to me, along with a warning that this was "time sensitive." This effectively limited my ability to carry out sufficient due diligence. In fact, I simply did not want to miss out and doubted if I ever had the intention to carry out impartial research anyways.

I jumped at the opportunity. Leaped, actually. It was a lemming-like, off-the-cliff plummet. The euphoria was short-lived. As reality unfolded, I came to realize that the business was not as "sold" to me, and my minority investment position gave me little recourse for change.

It was a lost cause but a great learning experience. It made me appreciate that the "school of hard knocks" was a great training ground.

And If I Were You...

1. Take the time to carry out this self-evaluation. It can be quite a revealing exercise. Repeat the process every six months.
2. Be honest. Don't embellish your responses.
3. After you commence your "hard facts" business planning, carry out this self-evaluation assessment again. Repeat the process, and see if your conviction has softened or shifted in any manner. Both your self-evaluation reviews should yield reasonably consistent results.
4. The questions posed herein go well beyond the "hard facts" associated with researching, carrying out due diligence, viability analysis, risk analysis, and all the other vital tools business students and entrepreneurs are taught. These are of a softer nature, albeit just as critical as any opportunity feasibility study. Don't ignore them.

Launching and Funding a Business With a Passion

Premise

After you have decided to move forward with your entrepreneurial dream, the real work begins.

Conventional Thinking

Current thinking is that startups don't need a full blown, three-hundred-page business plan to do an effective launch.

One approach is that you should start with a mini plan, sometimes that nails the issues that the rest of the world cares about, and is packaged in a graphically enhanced format, with photos and other visually appealing trim. This is your door opener. Here's what your mini plan needs to include.

- *The Market*: Describe the market that you are going to play in.
- *The Problem*: What is the problem with the current market?

- *The Solution*: What is your solution? Are you disruptive to the existing way of doing things? Are you more efficient, cheaper, or faster? Why will customers want you?
- *Unit Economics*: How will you make money?
- *The Team*: Who is on your team and what experience do they bring?
- *Marketing Plan*: How, when, and where are you going to market?
- *The Competition*: Who is out there now, and what are they doing?
- *Milestones*: What have you achieved to date, and what are the next "to do" steps?
- *Financial Projections*: A glimpse of the future. Is this a million-dollar company or a billion-dollar company?
- *The Ask*: What investment do you need? Lay it out plain and clear.
- *The Exit*: How and when do the shareholders reap their payoff?

The other lever that I always used was a great PowerPoint. Aim for a 10-slide show that only takes 15 minutes to present. That's usually all the time you'll get to pitch your company, if you're lucky.

What really matters is that your plan is "believable." Does it make sense? I once pitched an idea to a venture capital firm. They rolled their eyes and took a pass on my "crazy plan." They just didn't think it was believable. Within a couple of years, other companies had this product in every household in the country. This same venture capital firm asked me to join their Advisory Group that reviewed new technology investments for them. I could never get over that they passed on my pitch. I'm sure it was the *eye roll*.

Likewise, any plan that assumes that you will take over the majority of any market is generally nonsense. The same is true of plans that project dominance in a market that does not currently exist. Be real and believable.

Here are some other issues that you need to build into your reality checklist.

- *Risk Assessment*: One of the most effective ways to increase the *believability factor* of a startup is to take as much risk out of the plan as possible. To de-risk it. Startups are inherently riddled with risks, and these risks have to be identified and factored into the company's strategy. I once took a startup plan to an experienced angel investment group who fed it through their risk analysis process and shredded it. This was great. I got to see whatever they saw as overstated, understated, neglected, or just not factored in. We rebuilt our plan, developed risk strategies, and covered all their concerns. We became believable.
- *Scalability*: Scaling up points to an ability to rapidly grow your revenue without substantially increasing the costs. This may seem like an opaque issue, but it can quickly become a defining characteristic of any startup. Today's market demand can explode and you need to build that possibility into your plan.
- *Milestones*: A list of milestones is a great way to communicate that you are real. List all the baby steps that you have accomplished so far. They can be as simple as incorporating, filing a patent application, or hiring a key employee. Next, define the milestones that are on your to-do list. Focus, focus, focus really means deliver, deliver, deliver. That's the story that milestones tell.
- *Prototype*: In the time it takes to write a huge, weighty business plan, your startup markets may have changed and thrown your plan offside. Invest your precious startup resources into creating an early prototype. A great prototype, even if it doesn't actually work (mine never did), makes for a believable *dog and pony* show.

My Real-Life Story

Story #1

As the old cowboy saying goes, "never go to a knife fight without a gun." The same is true when you are pitching any new concept. You need your *good stuff* right out of the box. I once did a startup where I spent all of my time selling my story to potential employees, funders, and future customers. I desperately needed the good stuff to tell my story.

My solution was pretty simple. I got a professional writer, someone who could put the magic into my presentations. I scoured numerous young PR agencies knowing that they were all searching for new clients, and I found one that was willing to invest some free time into my business in the hope that I would become a paying customer down the road. They polished my PowerPoint, added focus to my web page, set up a media link and even issued some press releases that increased my visibility. In short, they gave me the *good stuff.*

Story #2

One day I was pitching an investor group and things were going really well, or so I thought. My presentation was all sunshine and lollipops, but my audience didn't see it that way. All they saw was risk on top of more risk. My presentation was a complete flop. This was a harsh reminder of why you need to "de-risk" your plan before you open on Broadway.

After my full retreat, I sought out a veteran investor to review my plan, identify the potential risks, and suggest remedies. I incorporated all of his suggestions into my revised plan. It changed the way we were perceived.

And If I Were You...

1. Don't waste your resources writing a mega business plan on day one. Rather, concentrate on an executive summary that deals with your business's critical issues. These are the ones that people want to understand.
2. Be realistic about your target market share. World domination is never a good plan.
3. Startups are full of risks, whether real or perceived. Identify them and build strategies to deal with them into your presentation.
4. Build a prototype, even if it doesn't work. It will help people buy into your vision.

5. Define your scalability. Nobody wants to invest in a house painting company that can only paint one house every week.

6. Find a good writer and let them polish all your public documents.

7. Brag about the milestones that you have achieved and highlight the ones that are on your to-do list.

The Absolute Need for a Minimum Viable Product

The Premise

Launching a Minimum Viable Product (MVP) can validate your business concept and establish you as a *doer,* not a *dreamer.*

Conventional Thinking

Too often conventional thinking advises you to build a totally functional version of your product or service and test it in your market prior to launching. This is usually an unrealistic expectation; it is, in fact, like putting the cart before the horse. It can be a disaster, mainly because;

- *You are building out a full product or service without testing whether you are actually responding to market needs and customer feedback;*
- *You may be forced to go back to ground zero to rethink and rebuild; and*
- *It's a lot easier to redo the foundation than it is to tear down the whole building.*

The solution to this somewhat schizophrenic expectation is the use of an MVP. An MVP is basically a way for you to present your product or service at a stage where it puts forward one basic set of features, for example "This is our product and this is what it will do. What do you think?" Its purpose is to collect feedback before releasing a full-fledged product or service. It's a form of research that lets you test the market before you dive into it.

The classic definition of an MVP is a version of your product that allows you to collect the most user data at the least cost. The MVP generally has enough features and sizzle to attract investors or early-adopter customers, while not actually functioning as a product or service.

Feedback from an MVP can shape the design and features that you can eventually build into your product or service.

The first smaller-scale MVP that I followed closely amazed me. It was set up by a group that pioneered the sale of pet food online. This was before people bought everything online with a simple "click."

Their MVP was out to prove this one simple hypothesis: would consumers use their service? That's the data they needed to validate. They launched a website that offered bags of dog food and cases of cat food, all brand name products at great prices. The shocking thing to me was that they didn't have any pet food, warehouse, or shipping partner and no way of processing transactions.

The beauty of this MVP was that they just wanted to know if consumers would accept their "concept" by logging on to their website and placing orders. This was the ultimate "lean" MVP.

With only a website and a little online advertising, they were successful in proving that their business idea had "legs." They achieved a real-world measure for consumer acceptance.

Here are several famous companies that used MVPs effectively. They all did MVPs in their formative years as a way to get launched.

- Airbnb. The founding partners used their own apartment to prove that their idea works. By creating a minimal website, pictures, and other details, they promoted short-term online rentals.
- Facebook started out as a simple messaging board posting system between college students. The seed was planted by their MVP.
- Groupon created an MVP by launching a simple WordPress site and PDF e-mails to early subscribers. The MVP proved successful.
- Other household name companies tested their business models by creating and garnering feedback and data prior to launching. These included Zynga, Pebble, Zappos, Etsy, Dropbox, Twitter, and even Amazon. All of them generated

simple, minimal-functioning MVPs with the basics of their business models and tested the market acceptability of their proposed opportunities. The rest, as they say, is history.

An MVP and a Beta Test are different.

- *The MVP may be close to being the first saleable version of your product or service, but with minimum features, and just enough to satisfy your intended audience. An MVP may also be referred to as an "Alpha Release."*
- *A Beta Test is more advanced. It is pretty well a final version for selective users to try under real conditions. The goal would normally be to polish up your market-ready product or service.*

At the end of the day, nobody cares what you call it. It's all about moving your concept forward. Focus on:

- Maximizing customer feedback;
- Building investor confidence; and
- Creating team credibility.

If you are in an extremely competitive space with lots of existing players, you may want to up your MVP to be "awesome" by adding a more than minimum feature set, a better design look, or enhancing user ease. Be prepared to tart up your MVP to broaden your user appeal and ultimately the quality of the data you extract.

Many of today's MVPs are promoted on YouTube and followed and commented on across all social media platforms. Heads up. You can glean a massive amount of valuable consumer feedback here; "I'd use it if it just had ...." or, "If I could use it to do...." Harness this source of data.

An MVP actually needs to be carried out, likely at your cost, before most third parties, such as early-stage investors, will take you seriously. It shows that you "have a dog in the fight."

MVPs can have a huge impact on your business planning process. In fact, they may determine the first major pivot for your company and often lead to a business plan update.

A successful MVP program can launch your business concept into the "real" world and if you don't get it right the first time, fine tune it and do it again. There is no limit on using MVPs as a form of research.

My Real-Life Story

The objective of the MVP I built for my financial services company was designed to attract consumers to try my service that had a great value proposition for them. Users saved a lot of money. The real trick (goal) was to gather data on the level of acceptance and uptake by retailers and the banks that processed consumers' transactions.

To accomplish this, we developed an app that consumers could use and then recruited some "test" retail outlets and one bank to support our MVP transactions. The whole structure was very much a closed loop within a small geographic area.

We were also shameless in coattailing on big name brands to operate our MVP. We used iPhone's apps, Amazon's AWS, Google Ads, and Mail Chimp, and not just because they offered the services that we needed, but because we could name-drop them to increase our own credibility.

This was not terribly expensive and was very doable. We were able to take a relatively complex business concept and "dumb it down" to a simple MVP. It proved our business and provided us with the validity that we needed. Our successful MVP moved us from the land of "dreamers" into the real business world.

And If I Were You...

1. Design your MVP around the data that you need to validate your business concept.
2. Remember, an MVP does not test a product. Rather, it tests a business concept. It's more about whether customers will use it than how it actually works.
3. Keep it simple and cost-effective as you will likely have to self-finance it.
4. Use big brand name companies to execute your MVP. Wherever possible, associate them with your MVP. This can help you establish credibility.

5. Your MVP data is a key element in your business planning cycle.

6. Do it early and include the results in your business plan. It will change how people such as funders and strategic partners perceive you.

7. Link your MVP to social media site and harness the resulting feedback.

8. Doing an MVP is an important step in developing a company. It validates your business plan and gives you credibility in the real world.

Critical Thinking and Business Planning Beyond the Norm

Premise

When it comes to planning your business, or presenting to investors, focus on what is important to your decision making, and to outsiders who you need as allies.

Conventional Thinking

Business plans are part of business planning, but there is so much more. This chapter deals with business planning beyond the "run of the mill," the kind of business intelligence that you and others can trust.

In the real world, these planning and presentation tools can paint a clear and concise snapshot of who you are, what your venture can deliver in terms of value, profits, and return on investment (ROI), and why others should take an interest in your company.

- *Value Proposition*
- *Revenue models*
- *Financial projections/proformas*

For your own planning purposes, these key business forecasts can provide you with the kind of insight that fine-tunes your decision-making process.

Value Proposition

Once a reader gets past the "what do you do?" they need to see your value proposition, that is, how customers define your value. Avoiding any semblance of exaggerated superlatives (e.g., amazing, best, miraculous, impossible to fail), your value must respond to the following in a clear, concise message.

- *Why are customers going to engage you, or buy from your company?*
- *What is your intended marketplace?*
- *Are you better, cheaper, faster, bigger, or more efficient?*
- *Why will you be successful, and can you prove it?*
- *How are you better than competitors?*

Whenever someone asks you what you do, they are seeking out your value proposition, that is why you are in business. Your answer has to be compelling, brutally honest, and backed up by solid research. Without a solid value proposition, there is no business.

I was once involved in a project that revolved around this exact question: Why will your customers buy your service? The answer was in the research we did through industry associations that showed that we could offer a service to existing companies for 30% of what it was currently costing them to do it themselves. We then wrapped this massive savings offer in a "no risk marketing package" and had a strong value proposition for our company and our customers.

Revenue Models

Revenue models are the twins of value propositions. Think of the two of them as Romulus and Remus. A great idea always needs to answer the "how do you make money?" question.

Business concepts are only awesome if they can make money. Otherwise, they dwell in the land of dreamers with dysfunctional ideas, like the bin of broken toys in Santa's workshop. A great revenue model predicts and justifies the results when the rubber meets the road.

My approach on money is very old school. I want to see a transactional revenue model. That is one with all the associated costs that go into producing a single unit of product or service, the price that it is going to be sold for, and how you make money.

The discipline in putting these "simple" models together becomes a cornerstone of your plan that illustrates a money-making endeavor.

Financial Proformas

Everybody loves proformas but, too often, readers don't believe them or are suspicious of them. Rightly so, since many proformas are written by businesspeople who are eternal optimists. Not only do your proformas need to be real, but they also have to be perceived as realistic.

Experience has shown that good business planners create three "what if" proforma models: worst case ("the sky is falling"); average case ("today is a decent, average day"), and best case ("holy cow, this is miraculous!"). This creates a more realistic proforma approach, encompassing a range of possibilities.

We have all heard readers' objections such as "your sales are too high," "expenses are always understated," or "your roll out is too aggressive."

There is another interesting and effective method of presenting financial forecasts, and that is by building "Stress Test Functions" into your proforma spreadsheets. The end user is actually invited to make changes to the numbers, and the results are discussed. It's highly effective and allows potential investors to actually take some ownership of your projections.

My Real-Life Story

The idea that some things are more important than others really hits home when you present your concept to a group of investors.

I once had the pleasure of pitching a concept to a group of angel investors in Seattle. They were hugely successful and had a very rigid format for being pitched. We were given only 10 minutes to make our pitch and not a second more. They actually had a person that gave you a "one minute to go" warning and then cut you off as the clock ran out.

With the pressure this format generates, you need to really zero in on the important stuff.

My presentation was simple and brief. After starting with a one minute "here is what we do," I focused on why customers would beat our door down (value proposition), how we make money (revenue model), and how profitable we would be (proforma financials). It was a three-slide presentation, and it took less than 10 minutes. It worked because it focused on the important features the group needed to hear and readily understand.

My presentation was followed by a tsunami of questions. Apparently, they didn't have a Q and A time limit. Their game, their rules.

The happy ending here is that they formed a due diligence committee and established a strong relationship with our company. This relationship was founded on our joint confidence in three clear understandings, namely, the revenue model, the value proposition, and the proformas.

And If I Were You...

1. Zero in on the most important issues in your business plan. Consider the big three, namely, value proposition, revenue model, and proformas.
2. Do your research and be prepared to justify and back up anything you say.
3. Use your research and 3rd party statistics as a way of validating your concept.
4. Separate your critical issues in your plan from the nuts and bolts of how to execute them.
5. Never use time-worn "feel good" statements to sell yourself or your company.
6. Using a sounding board you trust and who has no vested interest in the outcome of your business and let them play "devil's advocate" to find any potential gaps or shortcomings in your plan.
7. Think of these three things as the natural order of your business, namely, why do customers want this? how do I make money? how successful can I become?

CHAPTER 4

Resources and Foundation Building

Recruit Your Very Own Advisory Board

The Premise

Whether you are a new venture or an established business, access to intuitive independent advice will always increase your chances to succeed. That's where an Advisory Board comes into play.

Conventional Thinking

You shouldn't have to build or grow your business by yourself when there is so much entrepreneurial, management, operational, marketing, and sales talent to take advantage of. Create an Advisory Board.

Traditionally, you would look at surrounding yourself with a bunch of "wise owls." These so-called advisers are typically experienced businesspeople who can share their extensive knowledge and experience with you. However, in too many instances, the Advisory Board is comprised of "generalists." The conventional approach often falls short in delivering what you may need, especially with the tough calls that are on your plate today, and every day. You definitely need advisers whose expertise is specific to your own business interests, issues, and challenges. Focus, focus, focus.

The formation of an Advisory Board should be specifically geared to "advise" and objective insight into the challenges you face and the opportunities that present themselves to you. Comprised of experienced industry experts chosen by you, the Advisory Board can be an effective strategy that contributes directly to the growth of your company.

This is particularly true for early-stage companies that always face lots of hurdles and challenges across a host of business affairs.

Let's examine the difference between an "Advisory Board" and a "Board of Directors." The two terms are often used interchangeably but they are very different entities.

- *Advisory Boards are exactly as the name implies, "advisers" chosen by you, with no obligation for you to follow their sage advice, but it is eminently useful for you to use the members as sounding boards.*
- *The Board of Directors is a formal, legal structure that is responsible for the direction of the company and often comprised of stockholders and representatives from a business's funders.*

It is also important to nurture the relationship between the advisers and the company's outside directors, as there needs to be a level of compatibility for both groups to work together. That might include getting your Board of Directors to sign off on the makeup of your Advisory Board.

Generate a profile of the advisers you wish to seek out. The critical issue is carefully determining, up front, what you want, and what you expect from your advisers. Your real-time business needs and your critical near-term hurdles will determine what particular areas of expertise you need in your advisers.

Recruiting advisers is not as challenging as you might imagine. There exists a large pool of senior businesspeople who have an inherent interest to be involved in developing enterprises. Often, it is a "paying it forward" motivation.

Experience has shown me that every time I have approached someone to discuss their becoming an adviser to one of my ventures, they have almost always agreed to do so or opened doors for me to reach out to others, as in "you should talk to so and so."

Building and maintaining a relationship with all advisers (and would-be advisers) is an excellent strategy, as you can never have too many friends in business.

There are several other essential benefits of an Advisory Board.

- *Advisory Boards provide you with a unique opportunity to "test drive" your ideas, product development, growth strategies, or any critical matters where having a sounding board can help.*
- *An Advisory Board serves as a great way to get to know and work with people that you may want to add to your Board of Directors at a later date.*
- *Since Advisors seldom have any ownership in the company, there is no need to change the company's ownership makeup. This allows you to maintain corporate control. Your funders and investors will be pleased with that as well.*

Getting the most out of your Advisory Board demands a commitment of your time and energy on an ongoing basis. It is essential to regularly meet with them, as a group and individually, and to keep your advisers "in the loop." The more they know about your company, the better their advice will be.

My Real-Life Story

My business was developing financial technology products. When I was putting together an Advisory Board, I started off by throwing a real "Hail Mary," that is, a "why not try a long shot?" I targeted the recently retired founder of one of North America's largest lending companies.

After several failed phone calls, I finally connected with him. Initially, he was not very receptive to my pitch. However, all that changed when he realized that I was actually the founder that built my company, and it was actually my "baby." He immediately softened his stance and proudly shared the story of his successful "love child".

Apparently, when he started his lending company in a small town, nobody thought it would succeed. His wife didn't like his chances and even his dog kept growling at him. In spite of all the headwinds that he had to overcome, he grew his company into an industry powerhouse and eventually sold it for billions. That experience motivated him to advise my young company, and others, that exhibited big ideas. In the end, not only did I gain a great adviser but we acquired instant company credibility with him attaching his name to my enterprise.

There are great people out there who are willing to help you. Make it your job to find them.

And If I Were You...

1. Determine the areas that you want the Advisory Board to focus on and recruit experts in those specific areas.
2. Commit the time necessary to get the best value from your advisers. Keep them informed and focused on your goals.
3. Test drive your "new ideas" with your advisers. It's always better to get their input early on in your thinking.
4. Find a simple way to compensate your advisers. They generally don't need your money, just your appreciation and gratitude, and sometimes a good lunch.
5. To grow your business, you need good advice. It's your job to find your most compatible and useful advisers.

Cuddle Up to Some Powerful Big Brothers

The Premise

Establishing a working relationship with a significantly larger player in your sector is a highly effective way to utilize "big brothers" as stepping-stones to grow your business and gain some instant credibility.

Conventional Thinking

It's important to understand that well-established companies can only grow so much through "organic" growth, that is, growth that's driven by doing more of what they already do. Strategic growth by acquisition, licensing, or striking two-way relationships with companies that compliment and can deliver greater market access and market share are always of interest to major players.

Nowhere is this more evident than in the technology sector. Hardly a week goes by without a public announcement by a dominant industry stakeholder acquiring or forming an alliance with a fledgling company or startup, often for huge dollars. Their interest is twofold.

1. *Eliminating competition by purchasing them, as in the case of Expedia acquiring Travelocity, Hotels.com, Trivago, Orbitz, Hotwire, and others.*
2. *Filling gaps in their portfolio and providing instant access to growing markets. One example is Facebook's acquisition of Oculus, which provided the company a quick entry into the virtual reality (VR) business sector. This was far faster than Facebook trying to carry out the product development themselves.*

Big companies are always on the prowl for new opportunities to add to their stable. Their appetite is ravenous.

Every big company that you chose to target will have an executive, usually at the Vice President level, who is responsible for finding and vetting all things new. You just need to select the right target big brother and connect with this person. They will generally be quite approachable and as keen to find you as you are to find them.

You might think that it is difficult for an early-stage company to get the attention of a big player. It's not. Generally, they want to talk to you, and, just as important, they are fearful of passing on opportunities that their competition might pounce on.

You would need to be in a position to add value to the big brother, a well-established, highly recognizable stakeholder, whose product or service would complement yours, and vice versa.

Look for companies that share your values and can benefit by adding your product to their company or product offering. It's good to be wanted and needed.

Simply forming a working alliance has its own benefits for you. Strictly from a marketing and market awareness vantage point, use this relationship as a way to advance your own goals by coattailing on their name, brand, or customer base. The nature of early relationship deals is to keep it simple. Remember that their motivation is to see what you can bring to the table.

These deals can be as straightforward as an agreement to a limited test market as a way for both parties to measure each other. It also never hurts to mention that you won't be working with the big brother's competition while you are working with them. That's always a good point to make.

Don't try to formalize this deal with any sort of contract or letter of intent. They rarely work and usually complicate what you really want to do. The best you can usually do is a Mutual Nondisclosure Agreement whereby you undertake not to poach each other's employees or IP.

It's an interesting dance. Both parties can benefit from this kind of loose relationship and neither party is bound for the long term. Where you can really gain is by having your brand associated with one of your industry's big players, and that can become a major influence for your own growth and recognition.

My Real-Life Story

Story #1

I once established a relationship for a startup company with a major auto manufacturer. It was a classic little fish wanting to swim with a big fish. Actually, it was more like swimming in the shadow of a whale, who, in this case, not only built and financed autos but also operated a nation-wide dealership network. This was an ideal test bed for my little company.

To set this in motion, I visited the Business Manager at their local dealership. He then put me in touch with the Territory Manager, who then shuffled me over to their headquarters (HQ) person in charge of "new stuff." With one cold call and two follow-up phone calls, I was connected to the right person. This was a classic case of "stepping-stones" using one person to get to another.

I designed a product demo and arranged a quick trip to their HQ for a face-to-face meeting. We secured a simple deal where they got a first look at our product in action and we got to test drive our product via their retail network. This was a classic big-brother relationship. While they evaluated our product, we were able to access a great network to trial run an early version of our system. As a result of this relationship, we attracted additional investors to our company. Name-dropping helps.

For the cost of an airline ticket and a day in Detroit, the little fish got a relationship with the mammoth whale.

Story #2

In another instance, I organized a trial demo of a new type of media screen that also ran paid advertising. The trial run was carried out in a select number of independent coffee shops.

In the course of the test run, I received an inquiry of interest from the world's biggest liquor conglomerate. It seemed that one of their products was well known as a top-up to coffee, and they wanted to participate in our trial. This became a classic "big-brother" scenario. They had the opportunity to explore extending their brand's sales to new markets, and we scored instant credibility and recognition coattailing on their highly recognizable brand. It was decidedly win-win.

And If I Were You...

1. Establish a big-brother relationship that achieves credibility with your stakeholders.
2. Use the big-brother deal to increase your company's profile and attract other good people to your enterprise.
3. Always include a test or product launch that enhances your brand.
4. Be prepared to leverage your big-brother deal into other opportunities. You may not know what they are yet, but they will come.
5. Use these situations to jump start investment into your company.

Surround Yourself With People Who Make You Look Great

The Premise

A good team of management and staff reflect directly on you.

Conventional Thinking

Whether you are a fledgling entrepreneur, business owner, CEO, or manager, you will certainly find yourself building a support team. These people not only become your personal network, but they also represent you, and are a genuine reflection of you. Choose them wisely.

There are two schools of thought regarding the people you bring on board.

Surround Yourself With Talent	Surround Yourself With Puppets
Makes you look good to others	Reflects your own weaknesses, flaws
Fills your voids and gaps	Usually an ego-driven hiring
More time to work on what you do best	Takes lots of time to micromanage
Reflects upon your successes	Their mistakes become your mistakes
Effective delegation and downloading	Often become convenient "whipping boys"
Performance and results-driven	Difficult to delegate and then trust results
Able to capitalize on their ideas	Frequent staff turnover

Engaging staff based on their skill level is a viable strategy that can contribute significantly to the growth of your business. With decisive delegation of tasks and responsibilities, effective communications with each party, encouraging group dynamics, and carrying out adequate monitoring, you would be increasing your ability to manage or lead multifold. In essence, you replicate yourself and capitalize on the abilities and resourcefulness of those with whom you surround yourself.

Who should you include in your employee support team?

- *Plodders, those relentless souls who can take on any tasks, regardless of how mundane and tedious the workload might be. They trudge along and deliver what you need.*
- *Creative thinkers, who offer options and opportunities on issues and challenges that arise. They ask questions. They are positive and self-driven.*
- *Dreamers who have similar goals and aspirations that you do, and display the same "hunger" that you harbor. They are involved. They are dedicated. They see themselves as your clone. They feel part of your success. They want to be where you are.*

However, there is one major consideration overlooked far too often when a support team is being put together, and that is "personal chemistry".

Simply put, you need to like the people working with you. They have to "fit" your personality and your idiosyncrasies. They need to get your sense of humor, even if they do not share it.

Getting along is one of those qualitative features, impossible to really quantify, but critical in building a working, trusted relationship.

One suggestion for the key positions is to initiate a "honeymoon phase," a trial period that carries a broader perspective than "probation." It implies seeing how well you live and work together, how well you tolerate each other, and how the new person adopts your personal style, and, most importantly, your way of doing business.

My Real-Life Story

Aside from performance and capability, the personal styles and values of the people I surrounded myself with were always of critical importance to me.

Grant was a phenomenal researcher and door opener. His photographic memory made his research skills almost forensic. Prior to any sales meetings, I asked him to uncover as much as he could about the potential client and the person I was to meet. He was very much an "inside man," a relentless forager but with limited social skills and, as it turned out, with my wry sense of humor.

Liz was my Executive Assistant and my gatekeeper. She protected me like a mother hen would. She screened my calls and was astute and tuned-in to me to give me breathing room. She made sure I was not overbooked if I was exhausted, and even handled some of the staff beating their way to my office with questions. We understood each other. She was indispensable.

Jeremy was my strategic sidekick. I often invited him to join me at sales meetings, particularly with larger accounts. His style paralleled mine, but he was younger, savvy, and, most important of all, he was a great networker and glad-hander. He could spin tales, recite stories, and outlast any conversation of very little significance. He was a schmoozer, and that was a quality I had little patience for myself. Jeremy was my alter-ego and we made a great team. He knew exactly when to turn the floor over to me after he warmed up the audience.

And If I Were You...

1. Hire slow, fire fast.
2. Make sure your hires understand you, and you them. Focus on the qualitative side of people, not just the skillsets they bring to the table.
3. Wherever possible, try a honeymoon period where you can determine if you can live/work with each other.
4. Set specific targets and milestones for each person to reach, and hold them to it.
5. Assume most of your people will have some contact with your clients, suppliers, subcontractors, and related parties. As such, make sure you are comfortable with how they represent you, and the company. They are all your Austin Powers' "Mini Me."
6. Encourage group dynamics. Everyone needs to live together in your world.

Corporate Social Responsibility Is More Than a Catchphrase

The Premise

Enacting a corporate socially responsible (CSR) stance for your enterprise increases your credibility with your stakeholders, employees, and the community. It makes you feel good, and look good in the process.

Conventional Thinking

The adoption of socially responsible issues for your company is a low-cost, high-reward strategy. It is both the right thing to consider, and a smart thing to do. People like to be associated with "ethical" companies with a commitment to socially responsible causes or issues.

Many companies integrate CSR as part of their mission statement, often generated by their marketing people to augment the company's brand. While that is fine, the secret to successful CSR that delivers quantitative and qualitative results, is to actually do what you say you will do, and then show everyone that you did it.

Too often corporate social responsibility programs are created as "top-down" initiatives that are equally focused on corporate goals, such as reducing costs and driving new sales. These types of CSR programs are under constant pressure to justify their economic viability. If a company bases its CSR program primarily on achieving results to its bottom line, it will fail before it begins. The mindset is all wrong.

What may work for big business may not work for you. Young companies need to be more focused on increasing stakeholder support and building visibility and credibility in the community. Genuine CSR programs do just that.

Your business becomes associated with a "cause," you promote the worthiness of the cause that is close to your heart, and the "cause" promotes you as a "good corporate citizen." And your stakeholders are moved by your selflessness. Philanthropy sells.

The best way to find your corporate cause is to ask your employees for their buy-in on which third party organization that they want to support. A major consideration in this selection process should be identifying programs that are somehow related or parallel to the nature of your enterprise.

If you're in the food business, then you could consider sponsoring a Meals on Wheels program or a school meals endeavor. Make your social commitment relevant to your core business. Stay in your lane.

While your corporate sponsorship is a good first step, some of your employees will have deep passions for their own specific causes and organizations. Step up and support them. You can acknowledge their passion by simply allowing them to use some of the company's resources to support their cause. A simple allocation of some time, a computer, or office supplies can make a big difference and will be noticed by all your employees.

Not to be lost in this is your commitment to internal issues that cement a social and environmental responsibility. It's time to walk the talk. Formally adopting a CSR program into your company's DNA makes a big statement about who you are.

- *Don't confuse a CSR with a charitable donation. CSR requires you to be directly involved.*

- *It can be the little things that makes this work, like using recycled paper and low-energy light bulbs, getting rid of paper cups, or recycling everything possible.*
- *Establishing a social policy agenda is more important today than it ever has been.*
- *All these CSR baby steps result in a more positive work environment.*

These strategies are doable at any stage of a company's development and will generate returns in marketing, branding, with your employees, and with the client base you serve. It's worth the effort.

My Real-Life Story

Recently I had a mandate to set up a program from top to bottom, focused on engaging our employees and enhancing our image with our customers and in the business community.

My starting point was pretty simple. I assembled our employee group (about 15 people at that time) and challenged them to come up with a list of "doable" things that we could enact in our office. The key here was that they had to be affordable, so the suggestion that we move to a new "green" building was quickly discarded.

Using the "Think Global-Act Local" mantra, we easily came up with about 20 action items that we could put in place immediately. As a group, we were proud that we were making a difference.

One of our team was totally dedicated to supporting the local Society for the Prevention of Cruelty to Animals. She did fund-raising and even walked the animal shelter rescue dogs daily. I rearranged the office schedule so that she could support her passion, and we, as a company, benefited. We were the good guys who loved pets and stuck up for the underdogs (pun intended). Everyone won.

In another venture, our business was focused on developing systems for the financial industry. As our CSR, we chose to support a free consumer credit help service that was sponsored by a major bank. Our CSR fit our company well, and it didn't hurt our image to be on the same team as a big-name bank. And we got to help real people too.

Making a social responsibility commitment is now pretty well expected of all companies. It is definitely a "feel good" initiative. It is a huge marketing "plus" and it makes everyone involved a winner.

And If I Were You...

1. Always try to build your CSR program around your core business.
2. Support your people's passions. If they want to commit to worthwhile causes, so do you.
3. Get your people involved. They will be vocal about your CSR goals and commitments.
4. Use your CSR program as a networking tool to increase your profile in the community and the marketplace.
5. Use your "cause" sponsorship as a marketing and branding tool, extolling your participation on all your promotional materials and venues.
6. Make sure you get reciprocal acknowledgment from the organization being supported. This may sound mercenary, but it is a vital component of social responsibility, and all the players involved understand that "brownie points" keeps sponsoring companies happy.
7. There are hundreds of deserving nonprofits out there that need your help. Get on the right side of this issue.

CHAPTER 5

Leadership, and How to Be a Great Business Leader

Every Business Needs and Deserves Leadership

Premise

Leadership is ethereal. You can't touch it or taste it or measure it, but every good business needs it.

Conventional Thinking

Leadership is a kind of artform, and once you have taken on that role, you can't take a day off. If you're going to put on the leadership cape, you need to wear it 24/7.

Leadership is not a learned skill. You may not be able to learn leadership, but you can grow into it, and it is critical to building a budding startup.

Both leadership and management are necessary components to every company, but don't confuse them. Management provides an internal stability to a company, while leadership provides inspiration, both within and outside the company.

Leaders set the tone for the whole enterprise. They are the evangelists who totally believe in the dream and always seek an avenue forward and push on, no matter what. Most leaders understand what reality is. They just don't think that it applies to them. I'm a charter member of that club.

You need to establish the culture in your company. I used to be the first one in the office every morning. I'd make the coffee, take out the trash, and greet everybody with a "good morning." I set the tone with a "full speed ahead" attitude and everyone got it. That set the tone and the standard.

To get there, a leader creates, lives, and owns the big picture. Here of some of the "must do" items:

- *Set the table*: Create the big picture for your enterprise and establish a corporate environment that lets people grow, become better, and achieve great things.
- *Big goals*: Don't draw the map, but instead, determine the destination. Everyone wants to know the destination, not necessarily how you are going to get there.
- *Measure results*: Understand all the steps that you have to take to get to your goals. Define and assign them, and measure the results or failures. Fix what needs to be fixed, and then do it all over again.
- *Team meetings*: Make them a motivational event. Use them to constantly sell your vision to your team.
- *Use your advisers*: Make time for them. Mine their experiences.
- *Engage investors*: Always find out where they want to go and what their goals are, and build those into your own story, and keep your investors happy.
- *Own your style*: I use to take my team down to the waterfront where we sat on a couple of benches and planned our next moves. Find the style that works for you.
- *Build the team*: Be constantly on the prowl for talent. Court them, wow them, and hire them. Good leaders surround themselves with people that are better, brighter, and faster than they are.
- *Availability*: This needs to be one of your calling cards. Your team, customers, and investors need to believe that. My rule was that I returned every phone call or e-mail every day, and I responded to every team member as fast as I could.
- *Celebrate the victories*: You don't need to rent a cruise ship. Coffee and donuts or a glass of cheap champagne in the meeting room will work just as well. It's all about acknowledging

the group when it achieves a neat win on the way to the big goal.

- *A good second in command*: Every leader needs a side kick. Batman had Robin. Captain Kirk had Spock. The flip side of leadership is that other guy that actually makes the nuts and bolts work.
- *Become the "entrepreneur in residence"*: In all my startups I was the initiator, the visionary, and the early developer but once these startups became real companies, my role was over. I would become the "entrepreneur in residence," which is a nice way of saying "*he doesn't run it anymore*." The fact is that most great entrepreneurs are lousy operators. Find the person that will take you to the next level. It's part of the "leadership" thing.
- *Time management.* I always use the "*one-third rule*." I'd spend one-third of my time running the company, one-third searching for people that could help my company get better, and one-third of my time networking with customers, industry groups, and investors that could fuel our growth. Time is the ultimate currency. Spend it efficiently.

My Real-Life Story

Story #1

A good leader puts the welfare of his troops first. Everything else is second.

I once terminated a customer for abusing my staff. This was no small deal as this particular customer represented almost 10% of our total sales, but they also accounted for about one-third of our customer service issues. I never had an issue with their extensive use of our customer service group, but over time their interactions with my staff became increasingly nasty and belligerent.

The real win here was when I assembled our team and announced that I had dumped this customer. I made a big deal that I would never allow our team to be abused, no matter the costs. This was a big hit with everybody and turned out to be a long-term win for the company.

Story #2

As a young gun in a big company, I was tasked with winding up the operation of a sizable distribution center. The sad part was that a hundred warehouse employees were going to lose their jobs. Even sadder was that it wasn't their fault. This distribution center had just outlived its usefulness.

The night before I arrived at the warehouse, I had nightmares about how ugly this whole experience was going to be for all of us. It's not easy to be on either side of a hundred layoffs.

The best thing I did in this whole process was to get help from people smarter than me. In this case I seconded two people from the Human Resource Department at our head office. They got the state employment people into the warehouse to set up each person's access to benefits, wrote resumes for everyone, and even set up a 40-foot-long workstation in the warehouse so that people could job search, and we gave everyone time off with pay if they had an interview to go to.

Over the three months it took to roll up this warehouse, every worker found a new job. This story became an urban legend in our company. Our employees saw that even when events didn't break in our favor, we took care of our people.

And If I Were You...

1. Constantly be on the hunt for new talent to add to your company.
2. Find the person that you trust to run your day-to-day stuff.
3. Always be accessible to your customers, investors, and employees.
4. Create a climate where people can grow and succeed on a personal and professional basis.
5. Never let other people's version of reality limit your vision.

Business Rebels Are Business Builders

The Premise

Dare to be different. Being somewhat rebellious is a good thing.

Conventional Thinking

Business wisdom dictates that companies are launched under any one of the following scenarios.

- *Coat tail*: Ride on the success of a company by adding value to their existing product or service. One example might be the host of applications, cases, and bits and pieces you can purchase for your cellphone. These add-on ventures do not exist without a host. It's a very one-way parasitic relationship.
- *Copy and paste*: Replicate existing products and services already in the marketplace, with some possible improvements on features and price. The "knock-off" fashion, technology, and consumer products are extreme examples of copy and paste.
- *Leapfrog*: Using an existing product or service currently available, develop and launch a "new improved" model using others as stepping stones. This is a very common strategy in the technology world.
- *Business rebel*: Often referred to as "disruptive," the business rebel creates something that he or she thinks the market needs, but people don't know it yet. iPads, iPhones, and the Segway scooter are prime examples. The business rebel rewrites the rulebook and takes the highest risks for the highest possible rewards.

The business rebel represents the entrepreneur in the truest sense. Discarding the status quo, the rebel inhabits a world where business failures are learning curves that litter their pathway to that one great success.

Rebels often employ "elastic ethics" not traditionally taught in business school, acting more so on instinct, and developing their own rules by which the game of business is played.

That having been said, there are infinite shades of gray in the business rebel playbook. Some are innovators while others are instigators who often live by the mantra "go big or go home." To whatever degree, they are all disrupters.

In many cases, rebels do not necessarily have an innovative product or service. They simply may have developed a new branding mix, or a strategy by which to bring a commodity to market.

There are a number of characteristics that seem to be dominant in the makeup of the business rebel. See if you can recognize yourself here.

- *Everyone has their personal, emotional, and/or physical "baggage." Rebels own theirs.*
- *The status quo is a starting point. Rebels feel free to poke a stick in it.*
- *Rules are for the masses. Rebels know they can do it better and create their own.*
- *Rebels tune out nay-sayers. They have the strength to filter and focus.*
- *Business rebels make mistakes. It's all part of the pathway to success.*
- *Rebels recognize that timing is critical. An often-repeated mantra is "If you're not embarrassed by the first version of your product, you've launched too late."*
- *Successful business rebels don't expect to become stars overnight. They recognize that it's a process, usually one made up of measurable steps.*

My Real-Life Story

I was invited to partner in an outdoors adventure media series that showcased the beauty of North America's parks, rivers, and mountains. The photography was amazing. The hosts were charming and bigger-than-life. The settings were magnificent. All that was lacking was sufficient production funds and a broadcaster interested in carrying the series. Details, right?

The Asian tourism market was flourishing, and their interest in all-things-North-American was blooming. It seemed like a natural place for me to start. Using my network, I connected with an Asian broadcaster who had a viewing audience of 490 million.

I knew that "soft adventures" were the rage with Asian travelers who relished pseudo-danger outdoors experiences but needed to end each day with gourmet meals and Egyptian cotton bedding at their five-star resort.

With an impressive and highly tailored promotional package, I ventured bravely to the Chinese broadcaster's head office in Shanghai, meeting with their excited programming team. Apparently, I, as a foreigner, was a novelty for them, and I played on that asset. They offered me a Broadcast Agreement contingent upon my arranging advertising from North American companies who sought access to the massive Chinese outbound tourist market.

With a conditional Broadcast Agreement in hand, I returned home to secure advertising from government tourism agencies, tour operators, cruise lines, nature resorts, and hotels, all eager to attract Asian travelers. It was a case of leveraging the agreement from the Chinese broadcaster to attract advertisers, and vice versa.

Of course, there were challenges along the way from various Chinese "information control" ministries, but, in the end, the series ran successfully in China for two years. Everyone fared well, and our deal became the yardstick for other North American companies who followed suit.

And If I Were You...

1. Invest in talented people.
2. Keep it simple. It makes your ideas easier to sell to larger markets.
3. You don't need to be a villain to be a disrupter. Be nice.
4. Don't worry about trying and failing. It's part of risk-taking. Be unafraid. You only need one success to get stuff happening.
5. Stand apart by branding yourself and your company so that you attract attention and are readily recognized. Be unboring. Different is good. Outrageous is unnecessary and self-defeating.
6. Plan your milestones in quantifiable steps and celebrate as you reach and surpass each one.
7. Stay on course and focus on your ideas. You alone are piloting your business vision, regardless of the noise around you.
8. Run ahead of the group, but not so far that they lose sight of you.

Business Ethics Are a Moving Target

The Premise

Business ethics is an oxymoron and reflects your comfort in bending but not fracturing the rules and how you choose to carry on business.

Conventional Thinking

For many business ethicists, there is only one gold standard. Ethics must be unwaveringly honorable and virtuous, even piously so, as they apply to business. Business ethics operate at an elevated, highly principled level and are applicable to companies, managers, owners, Boards, Directors, and entrepreneurs. And all of us in the business world are obligated to uphold these haughty standards. There is no leeway given by those ethics standard-bearers occupying this rarified moral ground. This is black-and-white thinking.

Unfortunately, real-world business stakeholders have great difficulty blindly abiding by these conventions. Life gets in the way. The need to survive, cope, win, and lead, tests us all, sometimes quite severely.

Our fast-paced business environment demands quick reactions to formidable challenges and opportunities. So, we react, often without considering or weighing all the ethical fallout. That doesn't make us bad, just human.

There is, however, a viable middle-ground that accommodates an air of forgiveness. It's called "elastic ethics."

From a business perspective, elastic ethics are totally legal, predominantly moral, and highly effective in how entrepreneurs, managers, and companies can maneuver deftly in today's often chaotic business climate. They are edgy and somewhat rebellious in relation to the sober preachings of business ethicists. But they work, and are part of our makeup, whether we acknowledge it or not.

The lesson here is to refine your ability, and find your comfort level, to dwell in this in-between world. It becomes quite natural, and, despite the connotations here, you will not lose any sleep over any elastic ethics decisions and actions you take.

Elastic ethics are very doable and not nearly as onerous as they may sound. They are readily adoptable to whatever degree you are comfortable.

The best way to illustrate elastic ethics is by comparing them to cast-in-stone business ethics that occupy the majority of articles and books on ethics, social and corporate responsibility, governance, and boardroom decision making.

Issues	Conventional Business Ethics	Elastic Business Ethics
Trustworthiness	Accurately representing facts in all communications, candidness to build customer trust.	While trustworthiness is important, what is more essential is making people believe you are trustworthy, real or perceived.
Compassion	Kindness, care, and understanding relating to people, clients, and community, reducing any negative impacts of the decisions made.	Compassion and its related concern for customers is a component of elastic ethics. It implies broadcasting a real or fabricated attitude, but without any excessive guilt.
Diversity	Hiring people from diverse backgrounds, ethnicities, sexes, sexual orientation, and differently abled.	The people themselves matter more. Hiring is based on skillsets and work ethics, and the ability to deliver value to the company. Diversity is really a nonissue. People are people.
Fairness	Using honorable strategies in gaining advantage over competition, keeping fairness as a principle in all decision making.	Fairness is not a factor in a competitive environment. Winning is everything. If fairness is part of the equation, then it is fine, but not vital.
Exploitation	Exploiting workers in third world countries and exploiting tax loopholes are practices frowned upon.	Flexibly ethical corporate mission statements reflect a concern for exploitation of people and resources. However, it is often capitalized upon heavily in the company's market image and that is its prime purpose.
Law abiding	Assuring that all activities of the business and its key managers are well within the boundaries of the law.	Law abiding, by all definitions, is an important ethical priority. But, as with all other areas, the gray range between black and white is not forgotten and is fair game.

(Continued)

Issues	Conventional Business Ethics	Elastic Business Ethics
Excellence	Maintaining a high degree of excellence in all business practices, products, and services.	Excellence in products and services is universal. Excellence in business practices has room to roam.
Loyalty	Decision making that benefits people the company is loyal to, includes staff, stockholders, and customers.	Customers and stockholders are the prime loyalty targets, with staff following closely behind. Generating revenues and protecting investors and investments are keynote.
Integrity	Sticking with a decision that is morally right, demonstrating honor and bravery, even under fire.	Integrity is one of those ethically elastic features that has little earnest bearing other than "sure, we believe in integrity." Nothing to lose to buy in.
Responsibility	Creating a framework of corporate responsibility and accountability to customers, investors, and staff.	The number one responsibility is to generate a fair return to the stockholders and investors.
Causes	Financial and volunteer contributions to charitable organizations.	Any cause that can deliver positive sound bites for the company is a cause that deserves support.
Upholding brand image	Developing and continually maintaining a brand that is consistent with the core values of the company and its operation.	There is general agreement here with the conventional ethical thinking. Maintaining a consistent brand throughout the company and its operations builds marketplace recognition. The brand recognition is the core value being protected.
Sustainability	Commitment to respect the environment, use alternate forms of energy, decrease pollutants, and lessen energy consumption footprint.	Sustainability is going through a period of high visibility and importance to clients. Elastic ethics companies will promote sustainability, not necessarily because they genuinely care, but to enhance their image and attract customers.
Manipulation	Do not engage in manipulative financial practices, fraud, or insider trading.	Elastic ethics abhors illegal manipulation, but, as the saying goes, "figures don't lie, but liars' figure." Elastic ethics can surface where there is legal wiggle room.

Issues	Conventional Business Ethics	Elastic Business Ethics
Promise-keeping	Delivering what is promised, at almost all costs.	Once again, this is a motherhood statement, which, all agree, sounds great.
Profitability	Maintaining corporate profits, but only by cultivating high moral values and pursuing honorable business ethics.	Maintaining corporate profits. Period.
Leadership	Exemplary leadership by example and directing the management team to follow suit.	Leadership in any business is important. Leaders lead, are role models, and are part of the business's brand.

As you can see, business ethics can be flexible and highly self-serving. They dwell in the gray areas of ethics and are embedded, visibly or invisibly, into the very fiber of a high percentage of commercial ventures.

My Real-Life Story

When I started my business and economic development consulting practice, I knew I was up against some of the major firms in the industry. I needed an "instant edge."

I asked several high-profile contacts to act as Strategic Advisers, and I did not spare the opportunity to name drop.

I dredged up references from long-lost clients and business contacts, some of whom cost me future favors in return. Knowing that most clients never actually check references, I was doubly comfortable with these glowing quotes.

Whenever I prepared a proposal, I always bid a higher number of hours at a lower than industry rate, with the total dollar bid always being decidedly below budget. In my mind, I was working a contract price, so how I presented the time breakout was marketing, not hard facts. I knew the work would get done.

I always studied the client, their company, and their bid requests, searching out the hot buttons that needed to be pressed. This included meetings with the potential client to pry critical information such as their specific needs and expectations, both of which were often camouflaged within the proposal requests. I sought them out.

Within a couple of years, my company grew to offices in multiple urban centers with an exceptional team, and a portfolio of Fortune 500 clients. Elastic ethics certainly facilitated the early stages of growth.

And If I Were You...

1. Consider what areas you can afford to, or need to be flexible in, and govern all your actions and activities accordingly.
2. Never let greed entice you to break the cardinal rules. Stay within the lines, but walking along the edge is fine too.
3. Elastic ethics are not often taught in academia, or boasted about in the real world where it is generally, and sometimes unknowingly practiced to varying degrees. So, elastic ethics does not give you bragging rights that can come back and bite you.
4. Periodically you should review what is working and what is not and tweak your adoption of business ethics accordingly.
5. Business ethics, despite being cast in unwavering doctrines, are very personal. The degree to which you live by them is yours alone.

Perfection Can Be So Annoying

The Premise

Perfection can be a blessing or a curse.

Conventional Thinking

One would assume that doing something perfectly is, well, perfect! That is not really the case. Striving for perfection, regardless of the undertaking, does not always guarantee a flawless outcome.

Philosophically speaking, we live in a perfectly imperfect world. The idea of trying to be perfect is often a task without end.

In business, that can be reflected in launching a product or service well beyond its ideal introduction date, or starting or expanding a business after excessive planning and fine tuning, only to find that another company has entered and captured your intended market ahead of you.

It deprives you of the fast track, which can often represent your competitive advantage.

One example is the industry of high precision, costly audio amplifiers, speakers, and accessories. The day-to-day off-the-shelf components achieve a sound reproduction quality of about 85% to 90%, well within the range of the human being's ability to appreciate the music. However, those ultra-high-end manufacturers seeking to achieve the bliss of close to 100% are often lost in seeking perfection, and when they get close, end up selling into a miniscule marketplace that can afford "the very and priciest best."

I had such a client. They designed and laboriously manufactured perfect turntables that were works of art. In fact, their turntables were on permanent exhibit at the Metropolitan Museum of Modern Art. However, they also succeeded in driving their selling price tag of the turntable to over $25,000. They delayed new product market introduction sufficiently and gave the "every-man" priced turntables the opportunity to advance their own technology closer to my client's, but at a fraction of the price. My client likely achieved close to 99% perfection. But they closed their doors in the midst of yet another painfully slow and costly "next generation" upgrade to their product line.

The truth is that all entrepreneurs are perfectionists. However, it is the degree to which "perfect" is considered "adequate" that is the important milestone measure. Progress is often messy, and you need to develop a "good enough" comfort level or you may never "pull the trigger."

The "go–no go" cannot continue on forever. Ideas get tired. There is an outsized concern about making mistakes. Motivation wanes. Insecurities triumph. The truth is that neither too little nor too much perfection will lead to an ideal situation. Arriving at a balance is necessary for achieving harmony.

Settling for a reasonable facsimile of perfection is not failure. However, unreasonable expectations of perfection have the potential for failure, or are convenient excuses for possibly concealing any fear of failure or judgment. Perhaps some entrepreneurs and managers need to fail in order to educate themselves as to where to reset their realistic and achievable performance levels.

Often the need for perfection can be rooted in insecurity and uncertainty, coupled with a degree of personal lack of confidence or conviction.

If the need for perfection is rooted from the outside, there may be a fear of disappointing others weighing on your shoulders.

Here's how perfectionism can translate to failure.

- *By setting sky-high goals, there is no end to your undertaking.*
- *The risk level that you can endure is low. This is contrary to one of the entrepreneur's cardinal rules that risk is "acceptable" and tolerated in business. It is not often so.*
- *You work far too hard to try to please everyone, not just yourself. That is impossible.*
- *You may have a team, but you tend to micromanage and are uncomfortable delegating.*
- *You take your work seriously, which is fine, but you take any hint of failure personally. Remember, failure is not personal. It is an opportunity to do better next time.*
- *A heightened stress level stifles creativity, which then exacerbates stress. It is cyclical and self-defeating.*
- *You make mistakes but cannot accept responsibility, so you blame others around you.*

All that having been said, there are strategies to effectively deal with and compensate for your need to achieve a degree of perfection, and still allow you to gain a comfort level in that you are being as perfect as you can be, or need to be. They are detailed in the "And if I Were You…" as shown in the following.

My Real-Life Story

There are three stories worth recounting, each with a valuable lesson in companies striving for perfection, or not.

Story #1

A client had invented a device that assured the growth of planted saplings and avoided their uprooting by mother nature or grazing animals. These were huge and costly issues for large forestry companies.

I arranged for him to sell his technology to a forestry conglomerate, for more money than he had ever dreamed about. At the very last minute, actually at the signing ceremony at the lawyers, he backed away, insisting that, given another six months, he could perfect his invention even more.

The forestry representatives tore up his check and stormed out. My client kept fiddling with his invention. The forestry group commissioned a research lab to develop a similar product, which became an industry mainstay. My client faded into perfection oblivion.

Story #2

My client invented a toothpick. Not just any toothpick, mind you. It was a soft plastic pick, which could be impregnated with color and flavor. He engaged me to help him find investors to set up manufacturing the toothpicks. He was a bright, young design engineer who had no experience in production or marketing.

I convinced him to allow me to license the patented product to a large dental hygiene company. He acceded to my strategy, and a deal was struck. Today, he is retired, living on the royalty proceeds of his invention, enjoying the sun and the beach, with his two precious dogs by his side. I often teased him that he should rename his dogs Toothpick and Flosser.

Story (Almost Client) #3

This represents a case of setting the perfection bar below sea level. They invented something called a "ski-bike." It closely resembled a mountain bike but designed to race downhill on snow on skis mounted front and back alongside the tires. I was appalled at the very thought of this kamikaze device and asked repeatedly if it had been tested and perfected. I was assured it had been. I agreed to watch a demo at the local ski hill and was horrified when the inventor spring-boarded off a mogul, separating from his ski-bike and achieving an impressive height and velocity. I declined the contract to work with them. I hope he has since recovered and he has since realized that a little more perfection would have been useful.

And If I Were You...

1. Successful businesspeople and legends are known for their achievements and not because they were perfect. They were more than good enough. But they understood the value of timing. They knew that subsequent upgrades and innovations downstream represented almost limitless revenue streams. Try to adopt that kind of role modeling.

2. Do not beat yourself up for less than perfect performance. Shortcomings and even failure are valuable life lessons.

3. Accept compliments without making excuses like "if I had more time, it could have been better." It's likely good enough.

4. Learn to trust others around you. It's fine to micromanage, but do so productively. Impose your standards and ethics on your team without impeding their ability to deliver. Don't expect unattainable levels of perfection.

5. There is a difference between striving for excellence and holding out for perfection. Learn to recognize the two and set your targets accordingly.

CHAPTER 6

You Need to Learn to Deal With All Sorts of People

Doing Business With People You Dislike

The Premise

Sometimes you need to do business with people you may detest.

Conventional Thinking

We are taught that customers are "gold," and to treat each and every client as if they were the only ones on earth and critical to the survival and success of your business. This is what becomes ingrained in us and is repeated in the majority of "how to" business books. In fact, there are entire publications and sites expounding this doctrine. It becomes your mantra.

However, it is a half-truth. Yes, clients are important. They are the lifeblood of your business. That's a fact. But, how about if they are arrogant, disrespectful, or abusive to you or your people? Or how about if their personalities are so misaligned with your own that you cringe at any contact? (Other than invoicing. Invoicing is always a cure-all.)

How do you balance the "I need you" with the "I detest you"? As the comedian George Burns once quipped "Sincerity—*if you can fake it, you've got it made.*"

We all come across customers, or potential customers like this. It's almost like nature equips us with a "fight or flight" survival mechanism whereby we want to run, but we are hesitant to leave because we really want or need the business.

I have run into this with prospective clients who go out of their way to make sure you understand what a "favor" they are doing you by considering a business relationship with you. In some cases, I learned to "grin and bear it." In others, I walked away.

I was fortunate that, in my consulting business, there was no set pricing structure, and fees were almost always discussed toward the end of our meetings. The more the dialog went south, the higher I set my fees.

At the end of the day, you may likely work harder for an offensive client, and the situation will yield important lessons for you. The battle scars you might earn will serve you well throughout your business life.

My Real-Life Story

When I think back upon those demanding and demeaning challenges, I am amused that the context in which I lived through them is so different from how bemused I am at recounting the situations now.

Story #1

My company needed to quickly find a new bank. In this particular venture, we were in the service business. Our assets were our clients. Our current bank had changed priorities, and service businesses were now unattractive to them. It was a disheartening, unilateral move on their part.

I generated a phenomenal presentation package that highlighted our firm's excellent historical and current financial performance. We met in the bank's boardroom, obviously designed to impress and intimidate the bank's clients. It did. There were five bank representatives at the meeting, three of whom seemed disinterested (we were close to lunchtime). Needless to say, I did not like them.

In the middle of the meeting, a "shoe shine man" came in, decked out in a white outfit and cap, and started polishing each attendee's shoes. I felt like we were in a scene from *Gone with the Wind*. I was disgusted, but carried on, knowing full well the importance of securing the new line. We did, and my shoes looked great, but my perspective on life's class system shifted several degrees.

Story #2

In another situation, I was contracted to carry out a feasibility study on a proposed large cheese production facility associated with a major dairy.

We started each meeting, which included their CEO and advisers, with a sampling of cheeses. I should mention that I detest cheese, but fought back my nausea. Nor, obviously, could I refuse to join in. After all, the project was a cheese factory!

The "detest" part came in the form of one of the advisers; an arrogant, bigoted, lawyer with, seemingly, a limitless repertoire of stories and jokes abusing almost every race. He even referred to his new Jamaican daughter-in-law as "dusky," but he begrudgingly tolerated her because her father was high up in government.

He was tolerated by everyone because he represented the investors. He was not my client. I childishly taunted him by always addressing him by his first name, despite him correcting me continuously. This was obviously verboten in his world. His feathers were easily ruffled, and it made my involvement in the project a tad more tolerable.

And If I Were You...

Working with people you do not like or respect is probably one of the downsides of entrepreneurship or management, but it is vital in order to learn how to cope. I have developed a series of survival skills as outlined below.

1. Don't take any of this personally. Do not be drawn into any action or reaction that can impact the relationship.
2. Weigh out the likely benefits earned versus the likely abuse the relationship will dole out and decide if it's worth it. This is an important "go/no go" decision.
3. Understand and quickly identify why they are acting out like they are, and learn to play into it, to your advantage. If you feel flattery may placate them, then fawn appropriately, sincerely or otherwise.
4. Remember that the situation may not improve as your relationship builds. People seldom change. Respect your misgivings.
5. Playing "tag team" often throws the "opponent" off balance. Send someone else from your company to take them on at the next meeting.

6. Remember the end goal in any scenario, and that is revenues and profit. Never lose sight of the goalposts you set for yourself.

Mind Your Own Business

The Premise

Your customers' business is not your business.

Conventional Thinking

The concept of 'becoming one with your client' is impractical and naïve, and can put you into circumstances you may not want to be in, or privy to information you don't really want to (or shouldn't) know.

Business school tends to promote the concept of getting close to clients, earning their trust and confidence by positioning yourself within their inner circle, thereby making you almost indispensable. One of the trusted and sought after advisors. Close to the decision maker. A sometimes confidant.

In theory, that might sound like an enviable position to find yourself in, but the "Blinders Effect" will catch up to you. The effect is analogous to a horse wearing blinders that only allows it to see a few steps ahead.

Take the tobacco lobbyists who, knowing full well that smoking kills, still lobby on behalf of the industry, citing scientific studies, blatantly paid for by the industry, that claim the link between smoking and cancer is not yet proven. Seriously? Did anyone else see the Marlboro man, just before his death, speaking through his tracheotomy? The lobbyists remained oblivious, much to everybody's ridicule.

Therein lies the dilemma. Knowing too much about your client/customer can put you into a precarious position. So, do you do business, with some misgivings, with someone whom you have prodigiously researched, or do you ignore unpleasantries by burying your head in the sand? The choice is yours.

There is a gray area. Common sense would dictate that your business is yours, while the inner sanctum of theirs is theirs. That is the safer approach. There is no need to become conjoined with your clients.

Getting reasonably close is fine, but sharing too much information is perilous.

The same applies to what you share with others, particularly clients, insight about yourself and your company. Assume anything "business-intimate" you share can and will be used against you. That premise is almost a certainty.

Business school encourages building closeness between you and your customers but does not teach about "real world" business relationship-building and liaisons where being too close can translate to "lethal."

My Real-Life Story

There are actually two real-life stories worth relating.

Story #1

My client was a gold mining company with a somewhat aged and dubious claim and mine in Alaska. My contract called for news releases and Securities Exchange Filings, and I made sure that my contract read "based on geological reports and mining engineer-certified findings" provided by the client.

In the course of my relationship, I attended several of the CEO investor pitches, at which he always brought out a large gold nugget purportedly mined at the company's operation. It was always the climax of his pitch. Was it actually gold? I did not ask, nor care. It was outside my news release venue. As well, I was always curious about the millions of penny shares traded daily. Who were these "investors"? Once again, I did not ask, nor care.

My only releases were based on science. When asked to do a press release on something airy-fairy, I gave the task to one of their firm's in-house people and instructed them to keep my name off the release since I did not write or approve it.

As it turned out, the mine was real, albeit mostly depleted and barely worth the sought-after investment to rebirth the operation, especially in such a harsh environment.

As for that gold nugget, well, I never asked. But it was certainly big and shiny and made investors' heads swoon.

Story #2

Another client was a chicken slaughterhouse that processed 18,000 chickens a day. To me, that seemed like a lot of chickens.

The owner was a delight to work with. He took great pride in his mechanized plant and insisted I get a firsthand tour of the facility. Being somewhat squeamish, I declined, but finally, months later, succumbed to his tenacious requests. I was okay except for the carwash-style, steamy de-feathering room, and the entrails being packaged for a processor of chicken feed. It was the Soylent Green aspect that sealed the deal for me. I did not eat chicken again for six months. Nor can I still comfortably go through a car wash.

That having been said, our working relationship was excellent, and I delivered exactly what he had hired me for. To this day, chickens still haunt me.

And If I Were You...

1. Always be very clear what your role is in any relationship. As a service provider, be specific as to what you are contracted to do. As a products provider, detail exactly what you are selling and the terms involved.
2. Do not feel you have to become your clients' best friend. You are there to deliver, and while friendliness is fine, try to avoid crossing the line and becoming a confidant.
3. Learn as much as you need to about a client in order to make the sale and then to deliver in an arms-length manner.
4. Where conflicts arise, primarily in any kind of "insider" information being shared, redefine your role, in writing, give the client to someone else in your company to handle, or walk away.
5. There will almost always be gray areas that companies operate within. If you are apprised of them, and you are losing sleep, move on.

6. Avoid social gatherings and parties with clients where loose, liquored lips prevail.

7. Be the resource person clients can go to without also being their Father confessor.

8. Most importantly, work to find a model that provides a common ground for ongoing and workable relationships. There is always a middle ground without appearing disinterested or standoffish.

Where Do Your Business and People Skills Come From?

The Premise

Let's debunk the "nature versus nurture" attributes of entrepreneurship.

Conventional Thinking

Businesspeople display a series of characteristics, a temperament and a makeup that are the result of valuable academic schooling, experienced trainers, and, unfortunately, sometimes questionable "let me make you a rich entrepreneur the day after tomorrow" online snake oil salespeople.

The truth of the matter is that a successful businessperson, be they entrepreneur or manager, are an assimilation, in varying parts, of (1) training and mentoring (2) life experiences, (3) everyday life skills transposed to business, and (4) yes, genetics.

It is how you capitalize on these resources that will foreshadow your entrepreneurial success, or failure. It is within your control as to how best use the abilities within you and the glut of riches available to you. Don't settle for any middle ground.

The following represent the major skillsets generally attributed to each of the three source categories.

Learned business skills that are "nurtured" through training and mentoring are those that don't generally occur naturally in a nonbusiness environment. These are the main ones.

- *Delegation and effective micromanaging*
- *Objective, analytical research, without blinders predetermining results*
- *Effective communications*
- *Risk identification, avoidance, and risk mitigation*
- *Negotiating strategies and posturing*
- *People skills*
- *Effective communications and networking skills*
- *Team building and motivating others*
- *Financial management, on a corporate and strategic planning level*
- *Playacting and adopting a business persona*

Life experiences and every day skills are acquired as you grow up, confront challenges, interact, and socialize with friends and in school, and take on certain responsibilities at home, and include the following selective examples.

- *"Me first" thinking, assuring you are always number one in the pecking order. It is a survival skill learned early on*
- *Multitasking, since we learn to juggle any number of tasks and responsibilities all the time*
- *Personal and family budgeting and forecasting*
- *Respect and compassion for others, or, for those anti-social types, disdain for your peers*
- *Recognizing and dealing with competitors in school, sports, and in the painfully exciting dating game*
- *Relishing victories (or accepting failure and shortcomings) and learning to build on them*

Genetics dictate that success is also shaped by "nature," the presence of specific genes, according to some experts and studies such as the Duke University study published in the *Harvard Business Review* (January 2017). The study goes on to say that there are individuals whose self-employed parents or grandparents have a propensity to become entrepreneurs. Talent often flourishes in an environment that expects and, in fact, demands success for its offspring. Does this business-rich environment instill a predisposition for business success?

"Entrepreneurship by osmosis" can deliver any of these attributes.

- *Drive and ambition*
- *Confidence to try*
- *Leadership qualities*
- *Posturing and personal branding*
- *Risk taking, without the usual consternation and fear*
- *Character and persona development are definitely advanced stages of evolution*
- *"Absorption," the ability to learn as you go from those around you*

The conclusion is that, since entrepreneurs represent only 0.31%, or 310 out of 100,000 of the population, you find yourself in very rarified company. Your propensity for entrepreneurship comes from learned skills, life experiences, and/or upbringing, or some combination thereof.

For you, the determined entrepreneur, unless you have lived in a cardboard box all your life, you are not starting from zero. You likely have a solid foundation of learning, life skills, and genetics to build on, and the ability to access more resources during your entrepreneurial and business years. Never stop growing.

My Real-Life Story

There was a family owned, family-run business spanning several generations. Two sons from this "old money" family were raised in a highly privileged environment. Business was the mainstay of discussion around the dinner table as the boys, soon to be young men, were being groomed to take over the family business.

The brothers' succession was a foregone conclusion. Both were well educated, and enrolled in private schools and then into a university whose MBA program produced the best and brightest. Both graduated and entered the family business as executives. Their pathway to their success was predetermined.

They were the products of "nature," genetics, and upbringing, and "nurture," an exemplary education followed by experience in the family business.

Both pursued careers in the family business. Both married, had children, and vacationed where most dare not even dream of.

Both had almost identical advantages in life. What could possibly go wrong?

One went on to become the CEO of the family business and marched it forward to even greater success. The other drifted into a black sheep life of gambling, drugs, and divorce, and was disowned by the family.

The moral of the previous real-life story is, despite the best of intentions and advantages, life simply gets in the way. Success and advantage are sometimes yours to win or lose.

And If I Were You...

1. The "nature versus nurture" conundrum will not be solved today. The advice here is to do the very best with what you were given and have acquired.

2. Satisfaction of self is an important mindset that can contribute toward your business success. Work on it.

3. It is vital for you to continually generate a "Personal Balance Sheet" to identify what resources and business advantages you have accrued, through either nature or nurture, or both, and to use those assets to the best advantage possible.

4. If you weren't born (or raised) with a skill, be confident that you can acquire it. Take every opportunity to learn and grow.

5. It's fine to role model others whom you respect and admire. However, at some time, you need to become your own person and develop from within yourself.

6. We all have hidden, deep-seated talents. The true entrepreneur capitalizes on these and lets them blossom. Be that person.

CHAPTER 7

Money, Investment, and Partnerships

The Necessary Evils of Finding Money

Premise

Raising money for your venture is a necessary evil. It's not enjoyable, easy, or fast, but every venture has to do it. It will be the ultimate test of your personal strength and grit.

Conventional Thinking

No matter what you are doing, it needs to be funded. Many a great idea has ended up in the dumpster because it lacked adequate financing. Don't be fooled. Fund-raising is brutal and it will test your belief in your venture and your ability to withstand invasively close scrutiny.

Traditional thinking is that you launch your startup with the money that you and your friends and family kick in to get you going. It is a funding imperative that the company's founders need to have *skin in the game*.

The "friends and family" money is usually just enough to get your startup organized with a business summary, PowerPoint, website, and the things you need to go out and "sell" your idea to the funding community. Your next stop is the world of "seed" financing.

The seed funding realm is populated with a wide variety of "angel" investors who range from people that will invest solely because they like you and your idea, to sophisticated angel clubs that have more critical analysis and investment criteria.

If you find an angel who loves you and will give you the funding that you need, grab it and run, but know that this seldom happens in the real world.

Seed financing is a schizophrenic adventure. Most angel investors want to see a level of success before they invest. They want "traction," such as a market-ready product or real customers and actual revenue from sales. Your problem is that you need the seed financing to actually go out and do these things. This scenario leads to more failures than wins.

Enter *crowdfunding*. This is a viable solution to the traction issue and one that I've used successfully. It can straddle the gap between your own startup money and becoming "investor ready" in the eyes of the angels.

There are two types of crowdfunding that are appropriate with startups. Both of these programs have become very effective in raising that critical early money.

1. *Rewards* crowdfunding that lets consumers prebuy your soon-to-be product at a discount. This is a great option for companies that plan to have a consumer product that they can use as the bait to raise money.
2. *Equity* crowdfunding sells a piece of your company to the crowd and is better suited for startups or early-stage ventures that are not consumer-product focused.

One of the real attractions of crowdfunding is that it is relatively quick (can be three months to money) and it's actually not that hard. Once you have picked a platform (like Kickstarter) to use, your fund-raising program can be run through a website, a video of the how and why behind the endeavor, and a good social media presence. It's all done online and you can literally do it from your kitchen table.

Once you have successfully crowdfunded, don't take your eye off the ball. Forget the fancy office or new furniture. The only goal you have is getting the traction that you need for the next round of funding.

Now you are ready to go back to the angel investors, but be prepared. They will still have innumerable reasons for not funding you. Some of my favorites from my own experiences have been:

- *"You are too early—generate more traction."*
- *"You should have come to us earlier—we only invest in startups."*
- *"We only invest in companies within a 30-minute drive"* (I am not kidding).
- *"We like your deal but we are too heavily invested in your sector."*
- *"Get another investor and we might participate."*

There is no limit to the way angels can say *"no."* The good news is that fund-raising is like fishing; you only need to catch one fish to make it a successful day.

When you look into the crystal ball of funding options, don't forget these.

Partnerships: I hate partners but you never know when you are going to find a good one who can also bring funding to the table, plus, hopefully, other expertise and connections.

Joint ventures: I like joint ventures because you can fund raise off them in the short run and part with them later if they don't work out.

Mergers: You never know when you might bump up against another like-minded startup where it would make sense to work together. Two plus two could equal five and certainly helps your financing efforts.

Sometimes your funding opportunities can come from less obvious sources.

Law firms: Your corporate lawyer (not your brother in-law Bernie the divorce guy) can be a considerable source of funding options. They often have a number of clients and companies that are looking for new opportunities.

Accountants: The same is true with high end accounting firms. If they see a rosy future for your startup, they may introduce you to funding parties that you would never have imagined.

Incubators: Business incubators are great because angel investors circle them like vultures looking for their next meal. If you have a good enterprise, an angel will find you.

Fund-raising can be a scary journey but it is one you have to take, so buckle up!

My Real-Life Story

Funding your startup and networking are joined at the hip. The more you network, the better your chances are to secure a financing deal.

Story #1

I once was setting up a startup and I decided that I needed a funky office in an old warehouse district that catered to high-tech companies. I wanted to be one of the cool kids. Also, I hoped that it would help me attract some great people while being a fun place to work, 12 hours a day, every day.

So, I hired the realtor who had his name all over some vacant offices and I eventually found a great little space that I leased. In the process of doing all this, I explained to my new-found realtor friend what my startup was all about. His response was that he knew a couple of guys that would really be interested in what I was doing.

We set up meetings with each "guy" and within a month, each of them invested a million dollars into my startup.

Story #2

I was the VP of Sales for a company that was searching for its next-level financing that would let us expand our plant and branch out across the country.

Inexplicably, we got a meeting with a big-name fund manager. I actually knew his company because they sponsored skiing events around the world. I knew that he was a ski buff, and he visited every event.

The funny thing here was that I was a keen skier too and had skied at most of the international sites that he loved.

Much to the distress of the two company executives who accompanied me to this meeting, we spent the entire time talking about skiing and how much we had in common.

At the end of the meeting, he asked *"how much do you need?"* I answered *"five million."* It was in our bank in a month.

And If I Were You...

1. Don't be shy about raising your initial/startup/early-stage money from your friends and family.

2. Crowdfunding is a great way to bridge the gap between your startup money and a seed capital funding. Check out the different crowdfunding platforms to find the one that fits you and your business.

3. Use your early money carefully. Remember, you need to develop more traction to attract a serious investment, and that can be expensive.

4. Your professional advisers (lawyers, accountants, etc.) are great sources of funding opportunities.

5. Network with groups that will be the likely users of your product or service. You may find your funders there.

6. When fund-raising, be prepared for lots of rejections. It's the nature of the beast.

We Are Not Yet Done Talking About Partnerships

The Premise

Partnerships can be inspiring, or simply convenient or even painfully malignant. Choose carefully before committing. Partnerships can help you, or entrap you.

Conventional Thinking

Conventional thinking looks at partnerships in terms of legal agreements, governance and operational issues, share distribution, issues arbitration, and the possible termination of the relationship. Those are the mainstay concerns that common thinking generally deals with.

However, the absolutely most minor part of a partnership deal is the agreement itself and the legalities. While they are important, it is the "soft" elements of a partnership that dictate how well and how long any partnership thrives.

Business is "people to people" relationship building, and a partnership is no less so. There are so many key factors that impact upon a partnership relationship.

- *Is there a compatibility of personalities?*
- *What are your expectations of the pending partner, and how comfortable are you that they will be able to deliver?*
- *If your partnership is based on funding, what will the relationship be like after the investment is spent? What is the residual value?*
- *What other business ventures has the prospective partner been involved in, and were they successful?*
- *What power are you ceding to the partner, and are you absolutely comfortable in doing so?*
- *Does the partner have the time and expertise to take on the role you need them to fulfill?*
- *Do you have the same ethical business values?*

These are serious considerations that require forethought on your part. After all, you are considering selling part of your "baby" to someone who may be a stranger, or to someone you know in another context, like a friend.

There are some danger signs that you should also remain alert to that reflect problems percolating for your partnered business.

- *Dramatic disagreements on how to spend profits, or undertaking capital acquisitions, or even exit strategies.*
- *A change in the role structure of the partners, especially if the contributions of each become imbalanced.*
- *Outside interests that the partner may involve themselves in, particularly if it reduces their involvement in your business. The "shiny coin on the road" is often a distraction for investors, and aggressive businesspeople in general. It's only a problem if it steals attention away from your business.*
- *Issues that can't seem to get resolved, and the chasm keeps deepening.*

Partnerships can be a blessing, or a curse, and demands serious prepartnership screening and relationship-building.

However, once immersed in a partnership, where issues arise or peek over the horizon, they should be dealt with early on before any battle lines get drawn.

There is wisdom in the old "Law of Digging Yourself into a Hole" proverb that reads "If you find yourself in a hole, stop digging." Good advice for a partnership faced with divergent interest and intent. Deal with it.

My Real-Life Story

I have had the good fortune to have been blessed with one excellent partnership, one mediocre but somewhat lopsided partnership, and one "hound from hell." Luckily, I learned as I lived through my adventures, and my experiences and outcomes reflected my lessons learned and helped heal my battle scars.

Story #1: Hound from Hell

Early on in my entrepreneurial career, I sought out a partner whose contribution was to be funds for expansion. I did succeed, but once the funds were spent, there was little residual value left in my partner. I did all the work, he emptied ashtrays, made the coffee, and deposited customer checks that I had worked so diligently to earn.

I sought to buy him out. He was wealthy, and I was barely beyond pauperized, but my offer was fair. He rejected it. In fact, he told me his maid rejected the offer delivered by courier. Knowing he lived in a very fashionable neighborhood, I hired the Marshall Service, with roof lights flashing (for which I willingly paid extra), to deliver a second, much lower buyout deal in the late afternoon at the same time as his neighbors were arriving home from work. Needless to say, we settled quickly.

Story #2: Mediocre Partnership

While this partnership proved fruitful, and we grew the business together, the old adage of "people change" came into play. As our success grew, the chemistry of our relationship changed. He became the "alpha male" in the business and with all his personal relationships as well. We went from being friends to business associates, and from there to protagonists. The partnership needed to end, and it did. I had learned my lesson well.

Story #3: Excellent Partnership

I strove to find someone with common interests and the ability to bring value to the company (and, of course, investment). I did find such a person, and, before committing to a partnership, we decided to simply work together, unattached, and to climatize to each other. We did. We became partners, friends, and confidants. It was almost a spiritual experience.

And If I Were You…

1. Compile a profile of the ideal business partner, what you would expect from them, and the kind of person you would be comfortable working and sharing with. That should become your shopping list.
2. Never get into business with someone who is far, far wealthier than you are. Any kind of buyout or shotgun clause could adversely impact your ability to strike a fair termination deal.
3. When issues arise, or are about to arise, deal with them. Festering is an excuse for avoiding rapid resolution.
4. Make sure any partnership arrangement has an exit strategy that is not toxic to either departing party.
5. In drafting any kind of Partnership Agreement, chose a third party, impartial lawyer who won't sway the working relationship one way or the other. In my first partnership, I naively agreed to accept the use of the hound from hell's lawyer. The only termination clause in the agreement read "In the Death of Silverberg." That should have been a sign of things to come.
6. Before you tie the partnership knot, try a trial period to determine if you can function well together. The "soft" aspects of partnership cannot be overemphasized.

Rich or Poor, It's Sometimes Good to Come From Money

The Premise

Rich (and privileged) people are born with opportunities they can afford to waste. You likely cannot.

Conventional Thinking

It is often thought that wealth, particularly inherited prosperity, is a license to sloth. The premise is that the rich take their riches for granted, and, in many instances, this is too true.

There is a famous scene in the movie *Aviator* where Howard Hughes, in his formative years, is invited to his wealthy girlfriend's estate and during dinner, he is asked what he does. He explains his ambitious aviation ventures and the costs and risks involved. The mother says, laughingly, "We don't worry about money," to which Hughes replies, "That's because you have it."

There is ample evidence that many inheritance babies have little of the parents' business acumen in their genes. One would think they are from the shallow end of the gene pool.

For example, one of the key heirs to a liquor baron's fortune decided to divest his investment in a consistent dividend generator, one of the markets steadfast earners, and use the proceeds to purchase a money-losing major Hollywood studio. To nobody's great surprise, this ended badly.

A major department store chain owed its popularity, in part to its in-house well-respected brands of everything from expensively tailored suits to appliances. The mammoth store's high overheads could be absorbed by the inflated margins on these exclusive house brands.

Enter the heir. Raised in the elite business training academy called "family," one would assume that he would have absorbed the wealth and wisdom of his environment, but sadly that was not so.

He discontinued the house brands that made the chain famous, and, instead, he brought in the same lines carried by discount big-box retailers.

The results were predictably disastrous and the chain, and all its historical significance, met its demise through unchecked arrogance, stubbornness, and business incompetence.

I have met and dealt with several businesspeople who fall under the preceding scenarios, and it was strangely "entertaining."

Of course, success stories of the rich abound as well, but many seem to owe their success to heirs, following business models meticulously built and put in place by previous generations, or surrounding themselves with shrewd advisers.

And for the rest of us, entrepreneurship is somewhat of a privilege and offers membership in a club whose price of admission is hard work, creativity, and a willingness to take calculated risks.

The lesson herein is threefold.

1. *Money alone does not assure business success.*
2. *While we tend to comfortably adhere to older business models, tried and true for days gone by, that is an arrogant practice. Things continually change. There are always new lessons to be learned.*
3. *Most entrepreneurs do not have the luxury to waste opportunities and live to tell about it.*

My Real-Life Story

There are two experiences worth relating, one disastrous and one remarkable.

Story #1

One of my manufacturing clients had annual contracts with three brand-based underwear companies. This had been going on for 20 years, and the bond was strong. The product line was simple. Not rocket science at all. However, my client earned a bottom line of $1 million every quarter. Not shabby for a firm producing undergarments for just three clients.

The father passed away and left the business to his son. The business model and the client relationships were firmly in place, with little or no need to alter anything. The pampered son felt that he could do better than his father. Perhaps $1 million in net profits every three months did not meet the demands of his aggrandized living standards.

His attempts to renegotiate were a failure, and he managed to alienate his few clients. The company folded, and the three major clients formed a joint venture. They bought out the business for pennies on the dollar and kept the production lines humming without skipping a beat.

Story #2

A diametrically opposite example is worth highlighting. Another of my clients was a hard-nosed but soft-hearted business owner of a chemical company with sales offices across North America. His nephew was employed at the company, starting off as a shipping clerk while pursuing his MBA.

The nephew spent 10 years working through every position in the firm, up to the rank of VP Operations. I was present when it was time for the owner to retire. He ceremoniously tossed the keys to his nephew and said, "Your dad hired me when I was your age and passed the business on to me. Now it's yours, and you are very ready." It was a moving moment. He deserved it. He earned it. And it worked.

Interestingly enough, 25 years later, I had an opportunity to present to his firm. The nephew, now CEO, took my call and we reminisced about his ascent up the corporate ladder. He was now actually readying his own son to follow the same pathway.

And If I Were You...

1. If you are fortunate enough to inherit a company, or simply move up to a position of authority, don't try to change everything tomorrow.
2. A business that has shortcomings needs to be dealt with gently and firmly, like an iron fist in a velvet glove, but at the appropriate time, and after sufficient reflection.
3. There is a difference between wealth and power inherited years ago and the "new rich." The former command a modicum of respect. The latter are generally ego-hunters whom you can likely flatter and woo to gain advantage.
4. When doing business with someone wealthy, don't assume you are dealing with someone wealthy *and* smart.

CHAPTER 8

Marketing and Market Penetration Strategies That Actually Work

All You Really Need to Know About Marketing

The Premise

Marketing is an artform, and you cannot learn art from a textbook.

Conventional Thinking

Here's what is generally taught regarding marketing.

1. *Marketing* is the development of a strategy by which you build awareness of your product or service.
2. Your *Marketing Strategy* is your gameplan for delivering your marketing messages.
3. *Branding* is part of the marketing process. It makes your company memorable to your prospective and existing clients.
4. Your *logo and tagline* define and sell your brand.
5. *Advertising* is the mouthpiece of marketing.
6. *Promotion* is how you reach out to your clients and buyers.
7. Your *Mission Statement* is a sales job that promotes your image.
8. *Sales* are the measure of success of all of the above. Sales pay your salary, and the bills that fund the marketing, and the cyclical process repeats, and repeats.

While all of that may be true, learning marketing from textbooks represents a disassociation from the real world. The theory is fine but only to a limited degree and useful primarily as a starting point to understanding the black art of marketing.

So, now, put all of that well-intentioned academic book learning aside. There is really only one classroom that you need. Learning by real-world examples.

The Cardinal Rule: Very few business disciplines are as well shared as marketing. Your best classroom is what you see around you.

You certainly don't need to plunder or plagiarize, but you can deftly appropriate what aspects of others' creativity that you can morph and incorporate into your own marketing and branding strategies.

- *Research and role model others' campaigns that fit your products or services.*
- *Search out websites and social media pages that also epitomize what you are comfortable exemplifying.*
- *Learn from others. Coattail others' campaigns, imaging, and messaging. Make them your own.*

Marketing is the most visual aspect of business. There is so much out there to be shared. Creative and brilliant minds have crafted mind-blowing marketing crusades that can offer you the kind of invaluable insight you need to package yourself, your company, and your line of products and services. Why reinvent the wheel?

That's not to say that you should necessarily replicate what others have done. You should look to these marketing champions as idea-generators, perhaps one aspect or attitude that you can glean, personalize, and adopt as your very own.

If you research carefully, you will notice a certain commonality between competitors' campaigns. They say that every original creation has given birth to untold cloned variations.

- *Kickstarter replicated Indiegogo, the true grandfather of crowd-funding.*

- *In 1990, Nintendo held 90% of the video game market share. Sega adopted Nintendo's gamebook and captured 55% of the US market share.*
- *Apple, the undisputed champion of all things technologically amazing, accused Xiaomi of "theft" in copying Apple's smartphones and marketing practices. Regardless, Xiaomi is now the fifth largest smartphone maker in the world.*
- *Amazon released Echo in 2015, which preceded Google's Home device and then Apple's HomePod. The difference between the three in terms of function and target markets? Amazon was first, the others were copycats. The marketing campaigns of the three were (and are) almost indistinguishable.*

There are many more examples, but the lessons here are the following: (1) you can be a leader, which has inherent risks and high costs or (2) you can follow the leader. Research and learn how related companies, competitors, and even industry trendsetters have accomplished success.

My Real-Life Story

After having sold one of my businesses, I became enamored with the outdoors tourism market. This was clearly a high-growth, high-profit sector insofar as how I planned to launch it.

I created a high-end, luxury adventure booking agency, catering to a well-heeled clientele. By associating myself with elite lodges and resorts that had gained international notoriety, and offering tour packages to overseas adventure-seekers, I gained instant credibility in the marketplace.

My marketing was influenced by the very finest tour and resort operators in North America and overseas. It was based on the principle of "snob appeal." The more the adventures cost, the better they had to be. It was a convenient, high-margin model.

About one year later, a competitor entered the market, and they shamefully not only coattailed my company but they also replicated material from my website, pilfered the same customer testimonials, named their adventure tours identical to mine, and, well, it was like looking in the mirror.

It was pretty blatant, but I waited patiently until they had established themselves. I then approached them very amicably with a proposition, namely, buy me, on easy terms, or fight me in court for IP theft.

As a startup junkie always searching for the next new opportunity, I was quite happy to sell.

And If I Were You...

1. Decide how you want your company and products or services to be thought of and recognized in the marketplace.
2. Research direct and indirect competitors throughout the Web and social media platforms. Identify what you like about these players and how their creativity can positively relate to your own firm.
3. Engage an inventive marketing group to build on what imagery, brand, and promotional campaign you have singled out as attractive and possibly adaptable for your firm.
4. Test launch your marketing strategy. Make sure you are not mistaken for the company you "borrowed" from.
5. Once you have determined the viability and delivery power of your marketing framework, make it your own.

You Need to Reach and Impact Real, Flesh-and-Blood People

The Premise

Marketing is very people-specific. They are the ones you need to impress. Your sales depend on it.

Conventional Thinking

Suzie Homemaker was a marketing icon, for everything from appliances to cigarettes (remember those?) and household cleaners. Perhaps some of you do not remember the spritely, dedicated wife, cleaning and cooking all day in a flowing dress, apron, and heels and ready to greet her man at the end of the day, martini in hand, not a hair out of place on her coiffured mane and always tirelessly ready to please.

In fact, vestiges of Suzy are still around in those TV commercials with women dancing around the kitchen with mops in hand, scrubbing filthy bathrooms, and apparently, really enjoying it.

So, perhaps Suzie is not yet dead, but she is terminally ill and boring. We talk about her because she was a classic and a lesson in target marketing. Advertisers understood their customer base. It was the Suzie Homemakers who made the buying decisions in the households. That includes, well, just about everything.

Today's marketing venues are almost limitless, from TV and cable networks, radio (remember that, too?), and of course social media ads, blogs, and digital hawkers. The net result is that marketing today is more complicated, and there are so many more avenues to choose from. Every business needs to select wisely and cost-effectively and create corporate branding that is memorable. That implies highly targeted and enduring promotions aimed at a specific audience.

Target marketing is the precursor to sales. It helps generate revenues. No marketing = almost no sales. But you probably know that. My baseline definition of effective marketing is that it needs to impact people.

- *People are your clients. Not corporations, but the people with the decision-making authority to deal with you, or buy from you. That's who you need to get to.*
- *Generate an emotional reaction if that is the intent. "Appeal to the heart, and the head will follow."*
- *Surprise people to the point that they will relay their interest to others.*
- *Create a desire to buy, to be like that 18-year-old model professing perfect skin, to look like that perfectly proportioned, sexy lingerie model, to emulate that stud muffin to whom shaving equates to an erotic experience, and the button-pushing goes on and on.*
- *Speaking of hot buttons, marketing is most effective when it appeals to greed ("I want this"), ego ("This will make me a more important person"), sloth ("I can do this, but why bother if I can buy it ready-made"), pride ("People will be so jealous"), and presumed need.*

Marketing informs, evens the playing field between competitors by allowing creative, smaller companies to compete with "the big boys," sustains your presence in the marketplace, and continually engages your audience well beyond any past face-to-face purchases or transactions. Connecting, and staying connected, are of paramount importance. Don't get forgotten.

People can be influenced. In fact, they are infinitely controllable, and marketing is the driver. The 4P cornerstones of marketing are pretty straightforward. Before you launch any marketing activity, I suggest you step back and consider these factors.

1. *Product: What exactly are you selling, and to whom will you sell?*
2. *Price: What does market and competition research tell you where your price-points are?*
3. *Place: How does product marketing placement impact your ability to sell?*
4. *Promotion: How will people find out about you?*

There are a number of schools of thought for creating marketing campaigns.

- *Traditional: Kind of like the Suzie Homemaker approach, but if your product or service lends itself to a classic, time-honored approach, then this might be for you.*
- *New improved: Where you are basically saying "I have been around for a while, but I am so much better now. Check me out." It is somewhat of a dare to bring clients back to the fold.*
- *Personification: Used primarily in consumer-driven markets, this venue screams "try me, buy me and use me and you will become just like me."*
- *Rewards: Again, an age-old strategy that still works, and can include discounts, couponing, referral rewards, and even an invitation to join your "family."*
- *Snob appeal: One of my favorites is to price yourself high. People think that if they pay more, they are getting a better product or service. If need be, you can discount later.*

- *Need: Implies you are filling an identifiable gap that your client may have, or a need you are creating.*
- *Coattail: "If you like brand xx, then try mine," or "if you enjoyed your vacation at xx, we are right next door." You are capitalizing on someone else's better known product or service.*

Another of my favorites is *guerilla marketing*, defined by low-cost, edgy, high-impact, and creative tactics built on surprise. It ambushes and catches people off guard in their everyday lives. Carried out indoors or outdoors, or as a surprise at a scheduled event, these can be highly effective, and often garner a fair amount of free media attention. Here are a few examples.

- *Posters at a bus stop or bench that carry on a conversation with people.*
- *The stripes on a pedestrian crossing that get repainted as fast-food French fries.*
- *Manhole covers painted as cookies.*
- *Garbage bins painted as cans of pop or beer.*
- *Store or building doorways decorated as something being promoted. Two that come to mind are a gaping mouth marking National Dental Awareness Day, and, Prostate Test Reminder Day with the entranceway decorated as, well, you can imagine.*
- *Sometimes people themselves become the hosts for guerilla marketing. One of the most famous of all is Pamela Anderson in a sheer football jersey enthusiastically cheering on her favorite team at a game. The cameramen could not get enough of her, and she was subsequently "discovered."*

Social media is a techie world unto its own, including the impact of social influencers. Depending on the nature of your business, there are professional sites such as LinkedIn, Facebook Business, or Google, and there are more consumer sites such as Etsy, Pinterest, and Shopify.

For website building there is WordPress, Wix, and Squarespace, among others. Online surveys are best carried out by MailChimp, who also do online e-mail blasts, along with Constant Contact and others. And any decent website requires someone or something to drive traffic. Since visitors stay an average of eight seconds on your website landing page, search engine optimizer providers work to keep your website readily "findable" to site surfers.

Included in this witch's brew of social media are blogs you can write to keep your presence as upfront as possible. For corporate or product videos there is YouTube and the higher definition Vimeo. And for those inclined to more gossipy news, there is always Instagram and Twitter.

I sincerely doubt if that covers all social media providers. This is a field that eats its young, gives birth to new bundles of joy with unnatural clockwork and predictability, and is littered with hucksters. My strongest recommendation is to employ or contract a knowledgeable techie who enjoys the kind of bliss that only a confined space, a bright screen and a clanking keyboard can deliver.

My Real-Life Story

One of my own ventures was a tourism business with the humble moniker of "The Great West Coast Outdoors Adventure Company." It offered prepackaged, luxury, soft outdoors adventures (hunting was excluded), where the guests were immersed in experiences in which they felt that they were in some danger, but were not, and feasted each evening at a five-star nature resort, furnished with the finest of everything imaginable.

My target clients were middle age to younger old age adventure seekers, many reliving their days of wanderlust. Geographically, I chose the United States, Germany, the UK, Japan, and Canada as my prospective zones of interest. My research had arrived at that conclusion. I then prioritized my market penetration.

I advertised in foreign travel magazines and travel channels in my target markets. I produced and launched several HD videos that enticed audiences on Vimeo and YouTube, and on my website.

I sought out "multipliers," that is, companies that could refer clients to my business, for a commission, naturally. These included foreign-based travel agents, outdoors and hiking clubs, group booking agents, airlines, and adventure travel packagers.

I sold advertising to a number of select resorts who fit the stringent guidelines I felt were appropriate for my guests. As well, I sought out funding from the regional tourist boards where my host resorts were located. They were glad to pay as we were endorsing their regions as travel destinations.

I contracted with the resorts to pay my company upfront fees for advertising and commissions for bookings. If any of the resorts found themselves cash strapped, which they often did between seasons, I took my payment in holiday days, which I then resold.

The experience itself was an adventure, birthing a company from zero and building a series of marketing avenues that generated revenues, and a fun time as well.

And If I Were You...

1. Define your target market. Even profile your prospective clients. You cannot effectively market unless you know who you are selling to.
2. Be diverse in your marketing avenues. There are so many to choose from but only a small number will be appropriate for your company and type of business.
3. Social media, despite being attractive at being able to reach hordes of people, is highly competitive and crowded. Lots of advertising and lots of noise. Be cautious in choosing this as your sole avenue.
4. Wherever possible, carry out surveys to clearly identify client needs and determine how exactly you will fill those needs.
5. Test your marketing, either in a limited campaign, or a focus group, or, preferably, a beta test launch in a geographic location where failure will not spell disaster.
6. Track the effectiveness of any marketing campaign. You can do this with questionnaires or follow-up campaigns. Work out the cost of marketing per customer inquiry or sale.
7. Remember, the market is a moving target, so follow all trends and changes, including predicted future swings.

Growing Your Market Share by "Stealing" Customers From Competitors

The Premise

Assuming you are dealing with a finite market size, the "marketplace pie" is likely being reasonably serviced by others. So, how do you steal business away to create your own following?

Conventional Thinking

Perhaps the term "stealing" is somewhat harsh, so let's refer to it as "borrowing," because, somewhere down the road, a new kid on the block will be stalking you, and drooling over *your* customer base.

Classic market penetration strategy dictates that you work diligently to build a client base by effectively marketing your company and offering a combination of quality, price, and customer service, and any other perks you can think of, to maintain that loving headlock. However, those footsteps you hear behind you are disconcerting. Those are likely competition poachers tracking you.

The real strategy is to be different, innovative, slightly devious in your thinking and highly creative in your approach. The idea is to capture your market using nontraditional game planning, which also, incidentally, makes you a more elusive target for your pursuers.

Thinking "outside the box" is really about changing the box. This may not be for the faint of heart.

It's time to be more of a rebel, and less of an adherent to the same rulebooks that almost everyone is playing with. Here are some agitator strategies to consider, as well as some "warnings" of what traps you can inadvertently meander into.

- You cannot sell to the entire world. Carving out a specific territory gives you greater control. If you play in your own backyard, or pare out a controllable demographic in a region you can service, your ability to build loyalty will be greatly enhanced.

  When I was delivering workshops on doing business in Asia, I would often hear "We just want to sell to China."

My response was "Okay, let's see, 1.4 billion people, 22 distinctly different provinces in a country the size of the United States, many with very different tastes, levels of sophistication and market needs, plus intense government protective regulations, and at least five different language dialects. Which 'China' do you exactly want to sell into? Focus, people, focus."

- Consider creating a brand-new category for your business or products/services. Instead of copycatting or launching a next generation "new improved" product, work to package and market an entirely unique category. Keurig, Xbox, and iPads are big brand examples. Minivans and Greek-style yogurt are examples of new category products. While this route is expensive in terms of awareness-building, it is highly effective. You own the turf you create.

- Many companies attempt to cash in on the industry leader, riding on their coattails. The problem here is that you are encouraging your customers to keep dealing with the leaders. If you copycat the leaders, they must be pretty good. That is the customers' logical thinking behind this illogical market capture strategy.

- Look for the easiest opportunities to capitalize on, the ones that take the least effort, time, and money to win over. Even if the niche is small to start with, it can be the easiest one on which to stake your claim. Owning a high percentage of a low-hanging fruit is generally better than owning a single fruit tree in a far corner of a vast orchard.

- Learn to move fast and follow your gut instinct. Don't get burdened down with the need to compile mountains of data, metrics, and research. A true entrepreneur possesses a sixth sense and quickly understands the risks and rewards of taking action.

My Real-Life Story

I had the pleasure of working with a number of Indigenous communities, many of whom were in the midst of economic development to better the lives of their members. Entrepreneurship was considered a key driver in their quest for financial security.

In one instance, there was a particular community that had an expansive agricultural base. They harvested and grew a number of nutraceuticals, that is, plants, herbs, flowers, and foods that had some therapeutic capabilities. These were packaged and sold at markets and to health and beauty chains.

The Indigenous products themselves were good, but the competition was considerable, including a major industry player that had a track record of 20 plus years, highly memorable packaging and a recognizable brand that had been well advertised. Their retail shelf space dwarfed all the competition, including my client's.

I suggested they regroup and, instead of competing head-on, I helped them create a new category, "Indigenous nutraceuticals." The product line was repackaged under the new brand, "alterNative goods." The promotion included stories of the age-old properties that purportedly alleviated a number of health issues and conditions. *This was a new category with no current competition.*

Building on that, we developed a family of creams and potions for the natural healthcare market, riding on the same innovative brand creation.

The products themselves were really no different in composition and raw ingredients from the existing natural products that dominated the market. But the new category we created earned my client a greater retail shelf space allocation and a place in the chains' online and catalogue sales.

And If I Were You...

1. Use competitors' marketing, brands, and strategies as a jumping-off point and not a role model for your own company's products and services.

2. Before jumping blindly into any highly competitive situations, consider the risks and costs involved, and whether your pocketbook and personal comfort levels can bear the cost.

3. Focus on the attainable: territories, certain demographics, specific markets. Once you achieve that level of familiar business, then you can give yourself permission to go on quests to conquer bigger dominions.

4. Remember, everyone steals from everyone else. Unless you are creating a new product or a brand-new category, your existing and upcoming competitors will be sniffing around. Be watchful and stay one step ahead.

5. Go crazy. Think of alternate brand creation, guerilla marketing and explore new boundaries. Discard the ludicrous, but, guaranteed, somewhere along the process, there will be several "aha" moments that will generate strategies and ideas worth delving into.

CHAPTER 9

Branding Goes Way Beyond a Pretty Logo

Brand Your Business and Yourself to Intentionally Disrupt

The Premise

Believe in "Rebel Branding'." Break the rules, destroy what is not working, shock and disrupt the norm, and come out a winner. Be that renegade people talk about.

Conventional Thinking

"It is through disobedience that progress is made, and through rebellion" (Oscar Wide). In business, this applies to marketing in general, and branding in particular.

Standing alone means standing apart, and that is a good thing. You get noticed. People like rebels, perhaps, quite possibly, they would like to be one, but cannot or will not take the risk. It's out of their comfort zone, but they envision you, the renegade, as a winner. In their minds, they aspire to your level of rebellion, especially when they do business with you. And that is the ultimate and only point of these charades.

Traditionally, branding infers researching, designing, and adopting features for your company and products that customers will associate with you. It makes you memorable and builds awareness. It gives you an identity. It makes customers want you. And, as convention teaches us, it is all done by following a set process: get a great logo; write a brand message; integrate your brand into your company and products; think of a tagline to reflect your brand; develop brand standard guidelines; and stay true to your brand.

But you know all of that. That's "Branding 101." The real question is, are you a lemming (follower) or a leader (rebel)? The business world needs both, but the branding rebels are the leaders. Let's go explore farther down the rebel branding pathway.

There are three levels of rebel branding: company, products and services, and leadership.

1. Your *company* needs to be more than a provider or purveyor of something the client may need, fighting with umpteen other providers and purveyors, each claiming to be the best, cheapest, highest quality, when, in fact, you may likely be unrecognizable from your competitors. Find something or invent something that makes your business stand out in a crowd. It can be outrageous too.

   • *Buckley's Mixture has built an amazing successful marketing campaign around the fact that their cough syrup tastes horrible, but it works. They are not shy to keep repeating that mantra. It has become their rebel brand.*

   • *"Sweet Jesus" Ice Cream is in a populous playing field with majors and independents coveting a seasonal market. Their ice cream is okay, but their branding is outrageous and working. They claim that one taste of any of their ice cream concoctions will have you exclaiming their name in sheer delight. It is edgy. It is irreverent, almost sinful. But it gets attention and is highly memorable. It has helped them license stores throughout North America.*

2. Your *product or service*. What makes them stand apart? It's how you brand your products, and the trick is to keep it simple, and just keep repeating your brand message until everybody believes you.

3. Just look at Apple's *product packaging* that everyone is trying to emulate. It dresses up even the simplest tech gizmo and adds value to your product, and allows you to charge a premium as well.

4. And *how about you, the intrepid company leader?* You are the brand. People connect you to your enterprise, and vice versa. You are inseparable. You don't need to be a showboat, but you need to package yourself to first gain attention, and second, be respected.

- *Extreme rebel branding proponents create a cult-like, outlaw following. They believe in creating their own rules, and thrive on instigating change. Harley Davidson's "Screw it. Let's Ride" and "You Don't Need a Pinstripe Suit to Run the City" are examples of flaunting social standards.*
- *At the opposite extreme, there are "virtuous branding rebels" like Elon Musk and Steve Jobs, business leaders who present themselves as magicians, conjuring something up from nothing. They create value, but ultimately, they are extreme branding rebels.*

As a business leader, someone spearheading a company, you can adopt any one of a number of branded roles, from the "hero brand," someone who has overcome adversity, the "explorer brand," the innovator who won't accept limits, the "sage brand," someone dispensing advice and is sought out by colleagues, or the "magician brand," wondrously transforming ideas into reality. There is even a "save the world brand" whereby the company purports to be creating a product or service for the betterment of society. These are all admirable branded roles to adopt.

However, the "rebel brand" is the most adventurous, the most memorable, the most disruptive, the most theatrical in nature, and often the most impactful on the growth of your business. And, I might add, from personal experience, the most entertaining to engage in.

My Real-Life Story

I have always enjoyed undertaking a "front-and-center" role as CEO in my business ventures. Together with what some have called my "impish personality," the rebel branding was a natural direction for me.

At networking events and conferences, I arrived late and made sure I was noticed when I entered. In joining groups of colleagues, I often became the contrarian, taking on opposing viewpoints to entrench my position as a rebel.

I was often invited to speak at conferences and usually chose a topic and direction that showed some disregard for the conventional, and more so a disrupter, offering alternate strategies that shed a different light onto traditional thinking.

I worked very diligently to assure that this rebel branding did not make me an outcast but instead a sought-after counsel.

I instilled this thinking with my team, and every piece of promotion that was created for my business consulting company. For example, when we launched a division that sought government grants for our clients, our selling tagline was "Nobody Shoots Santa Claus."

Everybody knew we were rebels and likely capable of delivering results beyond what the other staid players in our sector could. They were right.

And If I Were You...

1. Don't accept rules that govern others. Find ways to leverage traditional thinking.
2. Theatrical training for selling will help you reach your rebellious character's comfort level. It may be who you are, or a role you are playing. Regardless, playacting is part of the process of establishing yourself in a certain role, rebel or otherwise.
3. Keep your brand message simple. That makes it easier to deliver and far easier to promote, be remembered, and, if necessary, defend.
4. The rebel brand often requires an overall makeover, including appearance and attitude. For some it comes naturally, while, for others, it is necessary to practice.
5. Persistence is good. Belligerence or backtracking means you have lost the rebel edge.
6. Find rebel brand role models to emulate. Follow their careers and rise to fame. Watch their body language, their attitude in dealing with others, the consistency of their message, and the fact that they know, regardless of what may seem contrary, that they are right.
7. Take on a rebel brand to whatever degree you are comfortable. Then push it a little farther.

Customers Just Love Stories: Be a Storyteller

Premise

Your story is a powerful marketing tool.

Conventional Thinking

Marketing experts have no shortage of tools with which to ply their crafts. In fact, between branding, digital, traditional media, e-mail, online strategies, and let's not forget advertising, there are 2.8 billion "marketing tools" websites offered up by a Google search. Just type in the keywords and stand back for the avalanche.

And for every strategy or medium, there are endless tools to measure the success of your marketing activity and suggestions to fine-tune your approach.

Interestingly enough, the one often overlooked marketing tool that can have the most impact is your story. Business storytelling relates to a story that impacts people, simplifies business information, and elicits a human response.

Your story sells. Emotions drive action far more than a logo or a bunch of statistics.

- *Who you are, especially because everyone's story is unique and likely memorable*
- *How you got to where you are?*
- *What inspires you?*
- *Your struggles and successes*
- *A steadfast belief in what you are doing*

These are just a few of the ingredients that make up your story. They are personal and can sometimes be painfully so. They are motivating. They become a critical part of what you are marketing and the essence of your brand.

Your story is how your customers associate you, with your products or services, and with your company.

The purpose is to evoke feelings within your audience. People become vested in your story. They relate to your struggles. There is a greater chance for the listener to connect with you and react by dealing with you.

There is a reason why charities don't talk about world hunger, but, instead, focus on the young orphan starving in the slums, and make sure you see the image of the unfortunate, helpless child. It's that story that gets people to pledge. Not to end world hunger but to feed that one waif at $2 a day.

Another example is the American Society for the Prevention of Cruelty to Animals and their drive to support the shelters and the excellent work they do. It's the pictures of a few caged dogs with their names scribbled on the kennel door that tugs at your heartstrings.

In business, the same marketing tool generates an awareness of your company based on a story. Your story. Telling your story and relating it to what you are selling is a relevant, effective, and timely strategy that not only builds a customer base but a loyal one too.

- *Personalization, that is you are the storyteller*
- *Authenticity (or a facsimile, if the story is to be embellished)*
- *A clear, thought-provoking outcome where the customer has learned from your experience*
- *An emotional connection with customers, highlighting how your story has impacted on what you do*
- *Getting your customers to relate to and buy into your story generates sales*

Business is people. Quite often businesses revolve around their owners. Storylines on effective websites, more often than not, include the life-changing experiences, visions, and inspiring adventures of the founders. Their stories sell.

Think Steve Jobs, Elon Musk, Tony Robbins, Bill Nye, Oprah Winfrey, and, well, I think you can see the power of personalizing and storytelling as part of a brand.

My Real-Life Story

I was contracted to work with a number of Indigenous (native) groups and organizations. There is one particular real-life story that comes to mind.

In the Inuit communities of the Arctic, survival is a daily challenge. The Inuit spirit has an inherent storytelling presence that presents itself through their art. Soapstone and marble carvings, paintings, intricate beadwork, and even unique wall hangings tell the stories of ancestors and beliefs.

Sedna, Inuit Goddess of the Sea, accompanies hunters venturing out on treacherous open water to hunt. Shaman masks, the Ice Spirit masks, and the war-like Tupilak Dwarf Spirit are but a few of the mystiques of the Inuit civilization.

For decades, Inuit artists struggled to sell their sculptures. In working with them, alongside a major art dealer, I encouraged them to tell the story of themselves, their community, and the spirits in their carvings. My instinct was that the stories were as valuable as the art.

Together, we helped shape a cooperative of Inuit artists, a highly recognizable brand, and an inspiring story that accompanied each piece. When buyers purchased the art, they were acquiring permission to share a dwindling and disappearing culture.

The strategy was most successful, and the artists themselves benefited from greater income for their communities. It has since developed into a lucrative business.

I have continued to use this storytelling strategy for many of my clients, regardless of their type of business. It always works. People love stories. They are "feel good" and motivating. As a marketing tool, stories cannot be overlooked as an important way to generate customer loyalty and repeat revenues. In fact, how many real-world stories throughout this book have you found memorable and relatable? That is storytelling marketing.

And If I Were You...

1. Every businessperson has a story to tell. Think about what led you toward entrepreneurship and what you experienced along the way. There is always some pain, humor, and inspiration in your history, waiting to be told.

2. Settle on the ultimate, clear message or moral of the story and build your story around it.

3. Find inspiration in your story. If the story is about your personal struggles, or is about parents, grandparents, or even earlier ancestors,

tell it anyways. The stories of overcoming struggles or the ingenuity of earlier generations can be motivating.

4. Don't give yourself the starring role as that can be construed as ego, and your message will be lost.

5. Work your storytelling into your brand so they become indistinguishable.

6. People like to be part of the story, so showcase clients' businesses as part of your story.

7. Embellish if you need to, but don't exaggerate. Make the listener focus on the solution.

8. Practice before you pitch to outsiders. Hone your message with trusted colleagues.

9. Always make sure the story has a happy ending that will make your customers feel good about dealing with you and your company. Perhaps you have noticed by now that "My Real-Life Story" sections offer up positive outcomes from even the messiest situations we have found ourselves in, and every "And If I Were You..." actionable items end with on a positive note. That is quite intentional. Always end with a high note.

CHAPTER 10

Sales Are Your Mainstays to Survival and Growth

Foraging for Leads and Business

Premise

I once had a daydream that my company had an absolute monopoly on a product, and I was being chased constantly by customers clamoring for my goods. Then, I woke up and realized, to my dismay, that business, for most of us mortals, meant constantly foraging for more clients and charming people to believe our pitch, and to trust us.

Conventional Thinking

Business runs on cash flow, which, in turn, is fed by writing business. It's one of those chicken-and-egg interdependent cycles that demands your constant attention as well as a fervent commitment to the creative pursuit of clients in order to keep "fueling the machine" called your company. This is called "foraging" for leads and businesses.

So, let's talk about foraging. We're not dealing with the "how to." The focus here will be which doors to knock on and the creativity that actually goes into the quest for clients.

Firstly, let's deal with the obvious, which, to many businesspeople, is not generally that self-evident. Instead of constantly chasing new clients, you should recognize that 80% of your revenues are generated by 20% of your existing clients. They are already fans. You have succeeded in winning them over, and, hopefully, shown them that you can deliver and are deserving of their trust.

Treat existing customers like family. Not the brother-in-law whom you detest or ignore. More like the mother who loves everything you do and say. Existing customers have loyalty. Count on it. Covet it. Do nothing to tarnish the trust.

The most attractive business model is where you *create clients as annuities*. They become reliant on you, or simply comfortable with repeat business, and they become part of your regular customer base you count on for generating revenues. One such example is insurance. Rarely does someone actually change brokers or insurers. In fact, it almost takes some sort of provocation to generate change. Customers stay with their agency year after year, and if and when you sell your business, that stable of loyal clients represents a significant value.

The beauty of annuity customers is that you maintain a base of customers, and that core group gets added onto continuously with new clients, year after year. For example, if you have 100 customer accounts in any one year, and you lose 20% the next year and gain another 100, your core group customer portfolio increases to 180. Carry that assumption through for 5 to 10 years and you will see how the customer annuity model outshines everything else. After a while, there is almost no need to keep selling. Your priorities shift to customer satisfaction and maintenance.

There are a host of foraging activities that are also very worthwhile to pursue.

Hunting. Attendance at trade shows, conferences, and other gatherings represent an excellent opportunity to sort through those present in relation to who is useful to you and who is irrelevant. If you have a high-profile presence such as being a guest speaker, your chances of attracting the right connections increase dramatically as you will be sought out as well as being the proactive hunter.

Multipliers. These are people who are not necessarily directly useful to you as clients, but they know others who are. They are door openers and any relationship with them should be pampered and protected. Don't assume lawyers and accountants are always within this category, as client confidentiality often comes into play.

Cross-referrals. Find noncompetitive players who service the same markets as you do. Set up a system of cross-referrals and cross-commissions or finders fees to encourage cross-pollination activity.

Joint marketing. In the same spirit as cross-referrals, there can be an opportunity to market and sell jointly with a noncompetitive player who also plays in your sandbox. Hotel and golf vacations, and flight and resort packages, are prime examples.

Media. Grab media attention where you can. Do press releases that are more than self-promoting eye-candy. Write for trade magazines, blogs, and social media platforms. Dare to be different. Make a splash. Be a rebel. Become memorable and get attention.

Distributors. When selling any product, find a distributor who calls on a host of customers in your marketplace, far more than you could ever reach one-on-one. As this relationship progresses, build a strong liaison with the preferred customers and adopt them as your own. While this may adversely impact the agreement with the distributor, their usefulness may have been outlived. Everything business-wise has a quantifiable life span.

The main take-away here is also that, when you are short of, or out of billable tasks, the previous techniques can be instrumental in filling up your work backlog. I have used and fine-tuned these to my advantage, and I can attest that they perform wonders.

My Real-Life Story

I had developed a line of nutraceutical products based on marine phytoplankton. It was basically a repackaging of an existing, certified supplement, but with a focus on the country's aging demographics.

The product was rebranded as "Baby Boomer Reboot." The promotional materials, Web, and social media all showed boomers behaving more like teenagers, complete with hijinks and playfulness.

While the product itself was great, and the chosen demographics was definitely a growing sector, the issue was getting Baby Boomer Reboot onto as many shelves in as many chain stores as possible.

The solution was linking up with a distributor who had the market reach we did not. They sold to health food stores, online retailers, and pharmacies. It was an expensive deal, but, knowing the costs in advance, we built the extra costs into our selling price.

The relationship was somewhat rocky but quite effective from a market penetration perspective. There was a personality clash with the agency's owners. Perhaps we just weren't accustomed to the assertive and somewhat obnoxious style of our distribution partner. But we all survived the honeymoon between our companies, and, as strange bedfellows, flourished afterward.

And If I Were You...

1. Having a great product or service is not enough. Use any and all resources and networks to secure a market share. Revenues count for everything.
2. Wherever you can, try to build a business model where clients become annuities. It is the ultimate way to build and, more importantly, maintain a loyal, repeating client base.
3. Build relationships with multipliers and others who can open doors for you. The idea of "using people" should not be foreign to you.
4. Don't go it on your own. Cross-pollination with others is highly effective. Distributors and sales groups have a role to play.
5. Protect your core customer base. They are likely the most valuable asset you have.

Taking on Work Just to Meet Cash Flow Needs

The Premise

"Cash-flow contracts or sales," you know, the ones you need but don't want, can work for you. They provide the revenues your business may need, along with some misgivings, knowing full well that there will likely be headaches or personality clashes along the way, or your ability to deliver may be impacted.

Conventional Thinking

In all my years in academia, and in all the business "how to" books I have read, from renowned university textbooks to get-rich-quick courses, there has never been any reference to "cash-flow" files. It's as if they do not exist, whereas, in real life, they are a staple of business.

What are cash-flow files? They represent contracts, commissioned work, or sales of anything from widgets to franchises where you just know, right from the onset, that they will be trouble. You sense it in the character of the client, or their corporate henchmen. You argue, albeit very hesitantly, that they are asking for something that will not really fill their needs, or deliver the results they are after. They should be considering item "B 15," not "B 1," but they don't listen and you don't dare argue the point lest they do not engage you, or buy from you.

So, you meekly and gratefully accept the contract, or sale, and prepare yourself mentally for the flogging that comes from an unhappy, adversarial relationship with a client. You can count on it. But you have their money, which you need because business is slow, or payroll or taxes are coming up, and, as we all know, a business marches on its cash flow.

It's almost shameful that schools don't teach you how to survive and even win with cash-flow files. They are a reality and common occurrence in entrepreneurship.

And, more importantly, you can effectively work them to your advantage. Here's how.

My Real-Life Story

There was a time in my consulting practice where the pressures of supporting prestigious offices and 35 highly trained, valuable consultants, further exacerbated by a slowing economy, became the bane of my daily "what are we going to do now?" existence. After some cutbacks and belt-tightening, there was still a looming cash flow gap.

A decision was made, by myself and my senior people, to pursue those kinds of files to which we had traditionally snubbed our elitist noses at, namely, cash-flow files. I was hesitant, knowing full well these contracts were generally distressful and often almost impossible to deliver completely and successfully, but common sense was overridden by a little something called "need."

Sure enough, one cropped up immediately as soon as we had lowered the bar. It was a study to be delivered in a region known for its NIMBY (not in my back yard) vocal influencers, who served on the Regional Governance Board. The generosity of the fees spoke to the bitter conflicts that I knew surrounded past efforts to promote change in a region where the tendency of some proponents was to build a mental high, spiked, electric fence with "Keep Away" skull-and-crossbones signage.

Any misgivings I had were readily overshadowed by the fee structure, which, I very importantly, negotiated to my advantage in terms of prepayment and progress billing, two cornerstones I had learned to build into all my dealings, especially the potentially murderous ones.

Sure enough, my first meeting with the proponent had the makings of the "perfect storm." The committee (I hated reporting to committees) was comprised of 12, unlike-minded people of numerous disciplines, from government and academia, to tradespeople and frenzied, but well-intentioned environmentalists, who had, for too long, been ignored. That was no longer to be the case.

I felt like the judge who will likely preside over the Theranos trial, and I sincerely hoped that I could find some common ground between them. It was a naïve but well-intentioned objective, especially delusional as I soon realized this internal strife had been simmering for many years, and I was but a convenient lightning rod.

Every time I presented to the committee, it seemed like another faction would spring to the forefront to criticize everything. It was like a "whack-a-mole" game, and I was the, well, you can imagine. One extreme example was, upon presenting a draft report, the committee member who was an aging high school teacher took it upon herself to correct my grammar. One sentence at a time. One page at a time. In a report of 175 pages, this an ordeal was beyond tolerable.

The next time I presented, amidst the tumultuous, bickering committee members, I stood up, extended my arms out to the side, and said, "Whose turn is it to crucify me today?"

Shocked silence prevailed as the group of combatants realized that (having already collected most of my fees), I had reached my breaking point. Things went smoothly after that, which brings me to a series of "And If I Were You..." I can readily recommend in virtually all sales situations. Yes, even "cash-flow" undertakings.

And If I Were You...

1. Make sure your mandate is clear. Be it the sale of your life, or boxes full of widgets, it is vital that the expectations are the same on both sides. These deliverables should be cast in quick-setting concrete.
2. Set out reporting lines. You are selling to a person (or persons), so don't let any peripheral intruders into the arena. It only causes dissent, and, far too often, offers others a soapbox to air their personal agendas.
3. Negotiate a payment structure that, if you have to walk away, you will not suffer any undue financial losses.
4. Deliver a quality product or service that fits within your corporate mission to perform.
5. Try to ensure that your client recognizes and appreciates your efforts. Some would call this "sucking up." I call it "insurance."
6. While you cannot ever prepare yourself for the unexpected, as that would be an oxymoron, you can assume that there will be friction. Some is expected, and is part of the process. But steer clear of any blood-letting battles, especially where you might be caught mid-conflict.
7. Always, always have a "Plan B."
8. Finally, never take any of these assaults personally. They are simply distractions. Just soldier on.

Keep Customers Ecstatically Happy

The Premise

Keeping clients as clients is so much easier than continuously hunting for new ones, so learn to really appreciate your customers. Tell them so, even the ones you may dislike.

Conventional Thinking

The cardinal rule of business is that clients drive your success. Building your customer base and meeting their needs to the best of your company's ability are keynote. These are often the cornerstone motherhood-type principles that govern mission statements and corporate vision manifestos. Maybe even yours.

Far too often, however, I have seen companies focus primarily on building a client base, when, in fact, this should be a secondary priority. I have been guilty of this as well. There is a false comfort in "numbers," whereby generating an ever-expanding client base provides you with a certain comfort level that you are doing well and your business is thriving. Wrong.

Your primary focus needs to be instilling loyalty in a select portion of your customer base. They represent the majority of the business you will write. Up to 80% of the revenues you will generate and over 65% of the repeat business you will enjoy typically come from about 20% of your customers.

Customer service is one of the key drivers in any business. It is more than marketing banter. It is a "thou shalt" commandment that needs to be integrated into the core of a business and into the mindset of your people, regardless of the type or nature or sector of your enterprise. Keeping your core client base happy should command your unfaltering attention.

On one occasion, when I was otherwise busy, I designated a senior team member as "VP Happiness." His role was to liaise with our key clients, entertain, and make himself "on-call" available. It was almost a disaster. My VP was good, but the clients wanted me, or my partner. They did not want to be shunted down the line.

This is actually an issue with large corporations, particularly service companies, where the sale is made by a senior salesperson and, once the deal is done, they hand off to their underlings. This can cause some customer resentment, or even "buyers' remorse."

There are some basic strategies to respect in regards to customer service.

- *Business is people to people. Never lose sight of the fact that you are not dealing with ABC Co, but with a human being who likes to be remembered and appreciated.*
- *Listen as much as you speak, and appreciate what your client needs. Chances are his needs will change over time, so be cognizant of that.*

- *If something goes sideways, take responsibility. The client will appreciate that you are human as well.*

My Real-Life Story

I was always a "socially conscious" businessperson, having served on a number of boards for organizations that supported worthwhile causes. Having my company as a financial partner to support these causes was part of my passion, and my vision.

We were inundated with contribution requests, all from very worthwhile organizations. So, how to choose and doubly benefit?

Business-wise, I achieved that with *"mirrored social consciousness."* I supported and paralleled the same causes and events sponsored by my major clients. Wherever they put their "corporate feelgood" dollars, I followed suit. My footprint was next to theirs. It was part of the bonding between my company and my most important customers and proved to be a viable strategy.

This represented a creative example of serving a customer beyond the scope of simply delivering a product or service to them. It appealed to a higher level of business social comradery.

Bringing customer service down to a retail level, where service tends to thrive or die, I had once received a gift that had been purchased from a home décor store. Upon trying to return it, I was rebuffed by the manager because the product was no longer sold there, even though it had been purchased at the store recently. She was arrogant and rude and steadfastly refused to budge. I explained that her stance over a $25 item was costing her a large amount of goodwill. I even explained I advise companies on this stuff every day. This was all to no avail. How often do you think I relayed this "horrible customer service" story to others? Years later I am still relaying this story.

And If I Were You...

1. Be nice. Imagine being on the other side of the desk, boardroom table, or retail counter. How would you want to be treated?
2. Gain some perspective. Take a temporary break from chasing new customers at the possible expense of ignoring your existing ones. Press the "pause button."

3. Get into your clients' heads. Find out how they feel you are doing, and what you might consider changing to meet their continually shifting needs. Use surveys and other feedback evaluation techniques.

4. Customer service that garners feedback by closely monitoring how you are perceived by your client base also generates opportunities for you in expanding, enhancing, updating, or adding value to your company's products or services.

5. Try to be flexible in your customer service approach. Some clients need handholding, others simply need to know you are there, some seem to need continual justification as to why they are dealing with you.

6. Instill an "over-the-top" customer service philosophy to everyone in your firm that has any impact on, or contact with a customer.

7. Respect the treasure trove called your existing client base.

The Creative Talents of Skating, Begging, Finesse, Dodging, and Faking It

Premise

There are certain skillsets that may not be 'pretty', but are critical for the survival of the entrepreneur. Among them are the artforms of skating, begging, finesse, dodging and faking it. They are not as ominous and devious as they sound.

Conventional Thinking

Artform generally refers to unconventional artistic expression, or any activity that exhibits or demands a high level of skill or refinement. Throughout this book there are numerous discussions about "artform," so let's delve into this some more, from a business perspective.

In business, artform translates to activities that go beyond the ordinary as they pertain to survival skills: salvaging unsalvageable situations, deflecting calamitous events, averting rejection, and/or absorbing body-blows.

They may not be the prettiest part of entrepreneurship, and certainly not the business-readiness skills taught, but, nonetheless, they are the kind of learned behavior that typifies the instinct-driven businessperson.

They represent the absolute refinement derived from life's experiences; relationships ended, jobs lost, being bullied, physical setbacks, conflicts with family and friends, and financial misfortune. These, and more, are the training grounds for honing your skills to survive, pivot, and move on.

In business, the core of the artform is the ability to react quickly, withstand challenges you encounter, sound sincere, and even win in the process. Overcoming adversity and finishing with a win is an indicator that life has taught you well, and you are able to adapt your life experiences to your business.

Here are some sample two-person dialogues that typify each creative talent. *(The client or other party portion of the conversation is shown in italics.)*

Skating

"Have you ever taken on a client this size?"
"Our clients cover all size companies, from startups to multinationals."
"Anyone else in our sector?"
"We do promise client confidentiality, but we are quite comfortable taking this on."

Begging

"You won't be sorry if you go with us."
"But what if you fail to deliver?"
"We won't."
"But what if...?"
"Give us the opportunity to prove ourselves to you."

Finesse

"Collaboration between our two companies can benefit both of us."
"We are your competitors."
"Not in everything, and not right across the board. We can help each other."

"I'm not sure we would be comfortable."

"Here's an idea. Where we sell different products to the same clients, let's coordinate our sales efforts, save money and realize greater revenues. That's a good start, right? Let's see if and how we can live together."

Dodging

"If our marketing group was more creative, we would have a greater market presence and a higher brand recognition."

"But you hired the best people around."

"Ultimately, the Board made the final decisions, and not all that I recommended."

"The Board does what's best for the company."

"Agreed. I understand that, but don't blame me when my hands are tied. Let's find a way for some autonomy for my group."

Faking It

"Your Web and social media presence are pretty solid."

"Thanks. Yes, we have spent a great deal of time and money to get there."

"What kind of hit rates are you getting?"

"Not enough. Never enough."

"We can build on your fine work to date and bring you to the next level."

The items highlighted above are simply sample dialogues highlighting the use of these skillsets.

The outcomes to all of these strategies are designed to deliver wins for you, or, just as importantly, pathways out of difficult situations.

My Real-Life Story

A close associate of mine was "volunteered" to represent her company, a large multinational, to join a workshop panel of experts. The subject matter was way out of her comfort zone and area of expertise, but, nonetheless, she had to be there, or lose "face" with her employers. It was a no-win situation for her.

It was a complicated subject, which I was very well qualified to address. However, no amount of cramming-coaching could provide her with enough material and insight to sound even remotely knowledgeable. She was frantic and distraught.

I came up with a solution. I had her call me on her cellphone but use a discreet Bluetooth device. I could hear the trend of conversation and questioning from the audience, and verbally fed her responses, which she repeated with great flair. She was a star!

In true classic James Bond style of wirelessly transmitting information to Auric Goldfinger during his card game in the movie *Goldfinger*, my associate and I managed to succeed in a number of cardinal entrepreneurial artforms: skating, finesse, and faking it. It was a hat trick!

And If I Were You...

1. The corollary is that humans have a "fear or flight" reflex. When facing situations that call for behavior somewhat out of your comfort zone, do not flee. Go with it. You will likely discover certain inherent abilities you have that will serve you well.
2. If necessary, I would definitely recommend working with a business coach who can help you shape rapid-fire responses to many of your business life's unforeseen surprises.
3. Most of us have a very strong survival instinct. Let it govern your actions. You would be amazed what you would do to triumph in any business situation.

My Mother Taught Me to Always Ask for What I Want

The Premise

Don't ask, don't get. So, please, go ahead and ask!

Conventional Thinking

Are you suffering from question avoidance, evasion, aversion, or phobia? Congratulations. You are part of a majority of businesspeople who are timid and hesitant of asking for what is often rightfully theirs, out of a fear of rejection or failure.

Perhaps it stems from your childhood and your stern parents, or the insecurities brought on by a date gone bad (admit it, we have all had those), or in business, being refused by a bank or investor, or chastised by a client. Whatever the reasoning, the simple act of asking for what is yours, or what you are entitled to, should not carry any stigma.

"Have you looked at that agreement"? "Is our check ready for pickup"? "Are you available for lunch on Wednesday and we can talk about the deal"? "Have you made your choice of contractors for that job (and when do we start)"? "Can you explain what you mean by clause 12"?

We tend to procrastinate in hopes of the answers arriving before the question is asked.

If you don't ask, the answer is already no.

The benefits of asking far outweigh the repercussions, real or imagined, of not asking. Plus, there are techniques and tricks to better your chances of hearing a positive response to your ask.

One of the best comfort-creators is knowing your audience. Before meetings, I would always research the company and the person(s) I was meeting. By getting to know them, I could gain their attention and support by being "one of them" by what I talked about, how I dressed up (or down), and most importantly, by determining beforehand how what I was offering made them look good, improved their bottom line, or fulfilled their desire to download what they abhorred doing themselves.

Always have a Plan "B" that can effectively shift the direction of the meeting or call but still maintain close proximity to your goal. "Oh, the check is not ready yet? Well, my driver will be in the area on Thursday, and I can get him to swing by." Or, "Just checking to see if that signed contract was e-mailed to me. We've had a few Internet hiccups recently, so I thought I would touch base."

You need to shore your courage up and ask as if you are expecting to get what you set out to secure. That level of confidence has a swaying effect on the other party.

There are other hidden tools that are also persuaders.

• *Use humor in your approach. It allows people to let their guard down.*

- *Make sure the person(s) you are dealing with are in a position to give you the answers you seek. Or, find out if they are the right person to be approaching.*
- *Don't sugar-coat your request, or dance around, or bury your ask in double-speak. Get to the point so the other party knows exactly what you want.*
- *Make sure the 'What's In It For Me (WIIFM)' motive is in place. "What's in it for me"? The other party will be more receptive when they see what they get in dealing with you.*
- *"No" is often a knee-jerk reaction, a way to move onto something else. Jump back in when they seem more receptive to you.*

My Real-Life Story

When I started one of my businesses, I sought out "multipliers," that is people already established in business who could refer leads to me.

I offered to cross-pollinate referrals, even though I was just starting out and had few to offer. I incentivized with commissions and finders' fees, but based only on consummated contracts because I had insufficient cash flow to pay advances. I charmed, and despite my charisma, I learned the meaning of the WIIFM principle. My spellbinding magnetism alone did not fulfill many of their WIIFM needs (i.e., ego, pride, greed, and sloth).

There was one firm I was particularly focused on. They were in a position to deliver a number of attractive leads, clients, and subcontracting work to me.

As prepared as I was for my first meeting with their CEO, the response was a rapid *no*. Picking up on this, I countered with *why*. It was because I had not been in business long enough, and had not yet proven myself.

I initiated "Plan B." I asked *when*, meaning what would it take to give him the comfort level to deal with me. He had never been asked that before, and genuinely let his guard down. He challenged me to come back in xx months with a client portfolio of xx, and we could talk. The gauntlet had been thrown.

I checked in with him, periodically, and we developed a friendly relationship, but the challenge had not been met yet. It was just to let him know that I was still alive and on track.

When the time arrived that I was now a "somebody," the work and introductions flowed, just as he had promised.

Interestingly enough, about six months after starting to actually work together, I had the distinct pleasure of telling him, in all seriousness, "Sorry, I can't take your contract right now. I am too busy." It became a standing joke between us.

And If I Were You…

1. Do your homework before any meeting or phone call or e-mail. Learn as much as you can beforehand.
2. Prepare yourself in terms of what you want to ask. Assume you have little time to connect before you lose their attention and their ability or willingness to listen.
3. Create and practice an elevator pitch if your foray is a sales call. It has to hit home and elicit a request for more information. Practice it.
4. See if you can role model anyone else whose style you are comfortable replicating.
5. Give the other party time to interject and respond. It will help you stay focused on your message, or require you to shift your thinking.
6. Stay on track during any encounter. Never lose sight of your intended end goal.

CHAPTER 11

Evolving Your Business

Capitalizing on Growth and Change

Evolve, or Get Left Behind

The Premise

Our ancestors wiggled out of the ocean and grew legs in order to survive and thrive. Their DNA evolved. Businesses need to evolve too. Make it part of your company's DNA.

Conventional Thinking

Traditional thinking stresses that you need to have a strategy to evolve. Companies need to change and grow in order to stay competitive and thrive.

Why is so much emphasis put on the requirement to evolve? It is a need to maintain market position, expand, better utilize existing resources, or, my favorite, catering to investor appetite.

Humans don't like change very much, but in business everything is constantly evolving. New technologies, market shifts, and hungry competitors seemingly materialize every day and accelerate your need to evolve. Think of this process as being "disruptive" internally. Question your own norms and always be wary of what might be happening in your own marketplace.

Companies can become static. It's like the law in physics where things at rest generally remain at rest. Companies can get like this too and need to break out of old, comfortable habits. Corporate complacency is a common pattern that you need to push back against.

The recent Covid pandemic certainly drove this point home. E-commerce and working remotely changed the way we live. We evolved. This time, Mother Nature dispatched the gameplan.

Too often, our efforts are limited to issuing the next generation of an existing product. That is not "evolving" at all. For example, when Apple launched the original iPhone in 2007, it was the first smartphone that allowed full access to the Internet. That's evolution. However, releasing version 12 of the iPhone is not.

Nowhere is it more important to have clear focus on your concept of evolution than for startup companies. The very nature of growing a startup into a successful business is the purest form of evolution.

Companies can evolve and grow by using a number of different strategies, but clearly, some of these options are better for young companies.

1. *Build it*: Organic growth is really growth that you generate internally. If you can create enough momentum, go for it. The issue here is whether organic growth alone can achieve your goals, and can this type of growth really lead to evolution, or is it really just doing more of the same? A "*more of the same*" strategy can eventually make you vulnerable to your competition. Here is a warning—this strategy can be time-consuming and expensive. Young companies need to find and allocate the budget to be able to afford this option.

2. *Buy it*: The acquisition of an attractive enterprise is another avenue. The acquisition of other companies is my least favorite evolution option. These deals always start out with the great expectation of improved efficiencies that will drive your revenue but almost never do. There are just too many hurdles to overcome to make most of these acquisitions work. Where possible, instead of acquisitions, aim for an asset purchase so you can leave the other company's corporate baggage behind and concentrate on your own goals.

   The *most cost-effective strategies* for young entrepreneurs are to "*borrow it*" or "*bundle it*."

3. *Borrow it*: Licensing deals with other companies are a great and affordable way for young companies to grow without taking on extra costs. There are lots of potential dance partners out there that will want to partner with you.

4. *Bundle it:* A great way to grow a young company is to combine your product or service with a complementary offering that your customers want. Whether it's coffee and donuts or software and hardware, two plus two can equal five.

Pick the strategy that best fits your situation and goals. There is no one right answer to your selection of a fitting evolution strategy. Pick what works for you and that may even be a combination of options.

Regardless of which of these strategies you adopt, it is essential that you remain open to the unforeseen opportunities that seem to pop up when you least expect them.

Evolving is a dynamic thing. Don't feel locked into any single situation. Organic growth can be ramped up, strategic relationships can be upgraded to partnerships or downgraded to supplier agreements, and your previous acquisitions can always be divested.

My Real-Life Story

Story #1

I worked for a company that had one major competitor. We were locked in a mature market and both of us used organic growth strategies to try to drive our businesses. We were like the corporate version of the Hatfields and McCoys. Neither would give an inch as we fought it out.

All that changed in a day. The owner of our competitor died suddenly and his company was immediately offered for sale. We jumped at this unforeseen opportunity and snapped it up. Not only did we grow but we evolved by adding new production lines and different products to our mix. We changed our strategy to evolve from "build it" to "buy it," but stayed true to our commitment to growth.

Story #2

I once pitched a new idea to a big corporation and I was amazed that they embraced my proposal so quickly. As a true entrepreneur, I'm used to push back from big companies. They often have an arrogance that is based on their belief that if they didn't invent it, it's no good. That didn't happen here. They loved our pitch and fast tracked our access into their company.

As we proceeded through different levels of this company, we found out why they bought in so quickly. In a seemingly parallel universe, they were working on the same "new" idea, but its development lagged ours. We were successful in jumping on this bandwagon because we had a working model of what was still a concept in their evolution policy. We became a perfect fit for each other.

They had actually created an internal mechanism to generate new ideas that would allow them to evolve. They encouraged each of their 10,000 employees to suggest a new product, a new system, or anything completely new to their business.

These ideas were fed into their "evolution" committee, and the best of them formed an agenda for a semiannual meeting at their head office. Each employee that had initiated one of the new ideas was invited to pitch at this meeting and the best of the best became part of the company's evolution policy.

They had a commitment to evolve and were open to a multitude of new ideas. In fact, they had committed internally to germinate new ideas and bring them to reality.

And If I Were You...

1. Pick a strategy that works for your company; build it, buy it, borrow it, or bundle it.
2. Ensure that your evolution strategy and corporate goals are synergistic. Both should "bump" against each other and go in the same direction.
3. Structure one of your senior manager's job descriptions to include analyzing evolution opportunities.
4. Set up an internal system that allows all employee ideas to percolate up to senior decision makers.

5. Be prepared to seize timely opportunities that drive your evolution.

6. Be open to mingling different evolution strategies if that's what it takes.

7. Embrace corporate evolution as a strategy to increase revenue. Make it part of your company's DNA.

Every Primary Business Has a Secondary Opportunity

The Premise

Your secondary business model can easily be far more lucrative than your primary operating business.

Conventional Thinking

The traditional academic thinking has always been focus, focus, focus. You have a business, or a new business challenge, and all your efforts need to be directed toward the realization, or continued growth of your existing venture. This is outdated "single-track" thinking.

The trickle-down opportunities, in many cases, far outweigh the value of your first-tier business, and it is critical that you examine every aspect of your enterprise to uncover its valuable gems. This demands long-term thinking and embedding different goal posts in your strategic plan.

In the "old" days, defined as pretechnology, companies built up client mailing lists, which they then rented, leased, or sold to other businesses that targeted the same client base. Any company that tracked and compiled a customer list found themselves with a valuable asset.

In those early technology days, these databases were utilized by credit card companies that virtually flooded the marketplace. Where did they get your personal information? Banks. Retailers. Census. Even schools played a role. I remember receiving a number of credit cards mailed to me during my university days, as did many of my colleagues. It was no secret where they got my name. What I didn't realize at the time was that educational institutions were profiting from my data, and earning revenues from a trickle-down benefit of sharing their student enrollment lists. I was part of their indirect revenue stream!

Moving on to our tech-centric commercial universe, WhatsApp launched its business model for free instant messaging based on "no ads, no games, no gimmicks." This was a deliberate, albeit costly launch strategy. But there was no benevolent thinking involved. They wanted sign-ups.

They built a massive customer following and a brand. Their database of users was highly sought after and valuable, so much so that Facebook paid $17 billion to buy out WhatsApp for its two billion users across 180 countries. WhatsApp was not a messaging company but a highly fixated data mining exercise.

Why are you in business? What are you looking to achieve? Selling time, expertise, or widgets? Not entirely. Think about how your primary business can generate a secondary one that can possibly dwarf the value of your principal enterprise. Think underlying value and work to achieve business success on possibly more than one level.

My Real-Life Story

I have good friends in Australia who were in the lighting business. They imported crystal fixtures from Eastern Europe and more commonplace home fixtures from China.

Their business flourished. They opened a lighting fixture manufacturing and assembly plant as well as a number of retail outlets throughout Australia's urban centers. They were a successful lighting industry player. However, their story does not end there.

The owners made a conscious decision that their strategic plan included real estate investment. They purchased the property for every retail store they opened and their factory as well. The retail rents they would have paid for leased properties likely covered the mortgages on the buildings they purchased.

When they retired from the lighting business, they leased out or sold all of their real estate holdings over time and had a steady, high-wealth retirement income stream.

Their lighting business was a deliberate vehicle for something much more lucrative. They were proud to admit that this success was attributable to thoughtful planning.

This provides an excellent lesson in creative strategic decision making, with a diverse end-goal vision in mind.

And If I Were You...

1. Look beyond the obvious and don't just be constrained by the immediate focus and daily demands of your business.

2. Right from the onset, think about what other valuable assets your business can yield. Data mining is one, yes, but there are many more: intellectual property (IP), licensing, franchising, and exclusive marketing and sales territories are just a few worth mentioning.

3. Design, build, run, and expand your business as if you intend to sell it for more than its valuation of hard assets. Wherever there is a possibility of generating second-tier value, it should become an important aspect of your planning strategy.

4. Develop a "spectator mode" ability to view your business from high up in the nosebleed section of the stadium stands. That can give you the perspective of looking more so from the outside as opposed to being locked in the grind below. How do others see you? What are you doing that might make you valuable to others?

5. Right from the start, identify other stakeholders or investment funds that might find value beyond your primary business, and continue to preen and groom your company toward attracting them.

6. Look around you. Follow your competitors and trade publications. See if anyone in your sector has developed secondary value for their businesses, which you can replicate in yours. Role modeling provides invaluable insight.

7. Assume that your client base, or knowledge base, or the proprietary know-how you have inherent in your business, may have a significant value. Protect and nurture it.

8. Find someone from within your industry who has capitalized on anything beyond the obvious, especially where that kind of thinking is applicable to your business. Hire them.

9. Think beyond the immediate. That is not always easy when you are immersed in the demanding day to day. Find the opportunity to rise above.

Pivot or Perish: A Key Strategy for Adapting to Change

Premise

While change has been labeled with different names like "resets," "retunes," and "reorgs," the current buzz word is "pivot," that is, changing direction of your business when you are out of sync with market needs. *Pivot or perish.*

Conventional Thinking

Traditional thinking is that all companies can thrive through their commitment to change, but this has never been my experience.

- *Small businesses embrace change and use it as a tool to grow. They "pivot" to accommodate change. A pivot is a one-time, nimble tactic that dramatically alters the direction of your enterprise. One example can be "I used the wrong software for this project and I'll fix it." It may take some effort and incur costs, but it is non-repetitive incident that can be remedied with a relatively quick fix.*
- *Big companies resist change and are usually slow on the draw. They generally "evolve" through a long-term strategy that supports their growth, but it is like a cruise ship instituting a dramatic shift off its designated course. It takes time, and the pivot is incrementally and painfully slow.*
- *I once pitched a big legacy telecom company, and during our conversation they explained to me how nimble they were. Nimble? I couldn't help thinking that this was the same dinosaur megacorporation that took a hundred years to make the phones work properly.*

Pivots are tactics that you, the entrepreneur, can use to carve out an advantage and out flank your big business competition. Pivoting also allows you to make your mistakes early when they are easier and less costly to fix.

You can't fake nimble. Startups have their own ecosystems that include innovation and nimbleness that allow them to pivot quickly and effectively. These are invaluable features of early-stage companies, and a major source of their inherent corporate strength. They tend to wield it like the effective weapon that it is.

There is a great deal written about well-known companies that successfully performed radical pivots, but it's important to realize that all these famous pivots were done in their early days. One of the most epic, industry-altering pivots was when Facebook changed from basically a college bulletin board to the social media platform that we all use now.

The Startup Renaissance

In 1960 a typical S&P 500 company was estimated to last 60 years. These days the average life span of a company is under 18 years. What happened? You happened! Startups have created a more robust and competitive marketplace and have changed this long-standing, staid dynamic.

The "Startup Renaissance" is what we are experiencing now. It is easier than ever to launch a significant startup with the tools that are available to you on day one. Right out of the gate you can be the "real deal," while building in the flexibility that you may need to pivot downstream. These of some of the ones that I have used:

- Amazon Web Services   Software development
- Google Ads   Online advertising
- Canva   Graphic design
- MailChimp   Market surveys
- HootSuite   Social media marketing management
- Slack   Streamline team communication
- Asana   Project management

Smart pivots that result from customer feedback are not setbacks. In a rapidly changing world, your ability to read the tea leaves and react quickly will better assure your success. People's lives have changed. How will customers deal with you in the "new normal"?

One of the most recent industrywide pivots is where bricks and mortar companies are going full out to establish online buying capabilities. They are doing so not only to adapt to changing consumer demands and unstable times (Covid-inspired home shopping boom) and to protect their market share, but to compete with the host of startups eating into their customer base.

The new normal has brought an incredible number of "pivots" into our lives that have become routine.

- Tele medicine   Now a standard practice
- Online groceries   One click and they deliver to my door
- Amazon Prime   Anything I need or want
- Online banking   Do they actually still have buildings?
- Zoom meetings   Who needs an airplane?
- Working remotely   Sweat pants and coffee!

It's hard to admit that you are wrong, but pivoting your startup is exceptionally healthy. Embracing a pivot demonstrates that you value the core components of your product or service, while understanding that you need to identify different ways to find your market.

My Real-Life Story

I once watched how a big established company tried to replicate a startup environment in order to develop and launch new products. It was a clever theory, but reality eventually stepped in.

They were in the business of manufacturing housewares and had lots of competition that were constantly pushing out new products.

Their solution was to set up small "startup" type groups within their mega company. As a new product was identified, they would assign managers from finance, operations, manufacturing, and marketing to act as the "founders" of this "new" company. Their sole job was to mimic nimble entrepreneurs and launch their new product ahead of any competition.

As clever as this concept was, the "founders" were never really entrepreneurs and their pay checks still came regularly from the big company. In the end, it didn't really help with their new product program.

Try as you may, you can't imitate the realities of a startup or early-stage venture. You need to be immersed in one.

And If I Were You...

1. If you find yourself failing, fail fast and go back to the drawing board. That's nimble.
2. Adopt the tools and resources available to you to launch your new endeavor.
3. Look hard at how the realities of a post pandemic world can change your business.
4. Reach out to your customers and learn from them. Serve their changing needs.
5. Your survival requires adaptation. It's truly a "pivot or perish" world for startups or early-stage companies.
6. Keep your head on a swivel and constantly look for new trends and technologies that can positively (or negatively) impact your business.
7. Keep an open mind when it comes to "change." It's coming your way. You can't stop it, and you need to harness it.

CHAPTER 12

Operating Your Business

Operating Your Business Means Controlling Your "Baby"

The Premise

Operating a business is crucially important but generally boring.

Conventional Thinking

Experienced entrepreneurs will tell you that creating and operating a business is curiously analogous to a romantic relationship.

Creating and Operating a Business	Equating to a Romantic Relationship
The "aha" moment when an idea flashes in your imagination	The tingly-touchy-feely courtship
Designing and planning out the venture	The engagement, complete with all the hopes and dreams you have for the future
Seeking out funding/investors	Shopping for the engagement ring you cannot afford and planting a few seeds of doubt
Launching your business	The honeymoon, where reality's starting pistol fires the warning shot
Operations	Equivalent to coming home from the office after another in a series of ho-hum days and finding a note that there is a tofu salad waiting for you in the fridge

However, the importance of operations cannot be overstated. Operations can make the difference between profitability and following a business model versus mayhem in running a business by putting out one fire after the next.

There are three schools of thought for styles of the entrepreneur founder.

1. *Do everything yourself.* This is very prevalent in early stage and sole proprietorship businesses, and leads to burnout because the owner wants to learn new skills in order to save money ("Sure, I can learn to do social media!"). By doing so, the entrepreneur steals time away from something they likely do best in order to learn to do something they know little about. It's a fallacy and a recipe for problems.

2. *Micromanage.* Assuming the entrepreneur has staff, or subcontractors, the owner will personally question every decision that others make that impact their business. This can be time-consuming and annoying and begs the question, why did you hire these people in the first place?

3. *Stand back and let it run.* If you have the confidence to engage your team members, then why not trust them to run things, under your watchful eye, of course? Regular staff meetings, progress reports, and updates can augment any insecure issues you may have.

There are a number of cardinal rules to live (or not die) by. Here are my observations gleaned by my founding and running a number of businesses, and learning to do things right, especially after I did them wrong to start with.

- *Keep negative emotions out of business. I am talking about anger, frustration, the need to vent, the desire for revenge, jealousy, and suchlike. They all color your decision making and anything done in haste may not be able to be undone.*
- *Control your cash flow. If you spend all your time chasing money, you can lose sight of your business. Tight cash flow issues create blinders for you.*
- *Deal with problems, including people problems, but do so rationally, and with a sense of finality. Get past them and move onto the positive.*

- *Try to keep things simple. The more complex you make reporting, paperwork, control systems, and accounting, the greater the likelihood of error and omissions.*
- *Delegate and set performance targets. Continuously challenge and test your people.*
- *Don't overlap responsibilities. The lines of authority and reporting need to be razor sharp.*
- *Stay fresh and stay current. Our world tends to shift under our feet. Things change. Actually, almost everything changes to some degree, so stay steady on your feet.*
- *When you get a nagging feeling about something or someone, act on it. Trust your instincts. You know the ones that got you this far. I sometimes had a misguided tendency to think "It will fix itself" or "That can't be true, so I will ignore it." You are hard wired to survive. Your entrepreneurs "fear or flight" response is keen. Pay attention.*
- *Finally, don't ever lose site of the big picture. What is that exciting end goal that motivated you to delve into the entrepreneurial world? What long-term goals have you set for yourself? Where do you want to be in xx years? Those dreams keep you going, day-in and day-out as you directly, or indirectly, operate your business.*

My Real-Life Story

I had a partner in one particular business venture where our skillsets and operating philosophies were closely aligned. However, another one of his exceptional abilities was sales. When we drafted our Partnership Agreement and outlined our respective areas of responsibilities, operations were on my side of the ledger and generating revenues was on his.

With this well-defined division of responsibility, I thought, most naively, that there would be little, if any, overlap. In the initial stages of the business, I was right. Then life got in the way, and reality has an annoying habit of planting seeds of discontent.

My people skills focused on team building, motivating and rewarding our staff. That was how I had always built a supportive and effective team that allowed a certain operational freedom that rarely proved me wrong.

With personal issues adversely impacting on him, my partners' people skills, it seemed, evolved toward intimidation and abuse. I only became aware of this when he started overlapping into my areas of responsibility and barking orders to my team.

My team was confused, but worse, I was livid. My partner and I fought daily. I led with my emotions. The company suffered and it came down to "it's you or me." He lost. In fact, everyone lost.

Operations, procedures, areas of responsibility, and control need direction and stability. They are, fact, fragile in nature and easily impacted by any contagion from a conflicting authority.

And If I Were You...

1. Set the ground rules and be very clear about how everything in your business gets done, from order taking to shipping, inventory control to record-keeping.
2. Create an Operations Manual that clearly depicts what procedures and controls are in place, and how they are dealt with.
3. One area of operations is price-setting and assuring your margins are acceptable. That is one area that needs to be regularly reviewed.
4. Supplier relations and maintaining supply chains as well as a bank of subcontractors you may be dealing with, all need to be nurtured.
5. Where you identify any weak link in operations, jump in to deal with it before it becomes a costly issue.
6. Operations extend to all facets of your business, including sales. Set targets for everyone and milestones for your salespeople.

Your Business, Your "Love Child": Control It, Run It.

Premise

Once you have launched your business and achieved your initial successes, the battle to maintain control of your *love child* really fires up.

Conventional Thinking

The reality of launching a new business is that the majority of startups fail within two years. To avoid this fate, it is critical that control of the company remains in the hands of the founders. More specifically, you.

It is the company founders and their team who are responsible for delivering on the business's potential and maintaining overall company control. You will likely need to compensate your key team members with some stock, attract investors who will want more stock, and increase your board, which will demand more stock. This is the juggling act that all entrepreneurs face while trying to keep control of their companies.

When you are approached by an early-stage investor who needs to own 51% of your startup, walk away. No, run away. Startups will succeed or fail based on the skill of the founding team and not the greedy desire of any investor to legally control the company.

Young companies don't usually achieve stability until they have their team rounded out, have built and launched their product or service, and have established a stable revenue stream. During this formative period, it is wise to keep a keen eye on the following.

- *Ownership.* You may own 100% of your company on day one, but after that, you will see it going out the door piece by piece. This is a necessary part of growing a company as outsiders get involved, but it needs to be tightly controlled. My mantra is that the founders and the key management group will drive the success of the company and this group needs to maintain a majority ownership during the business's formative years.
- *Board control.* You can own the majority of your company, but that might not mean that you have voting control of your Board of Directors. The Board can change the direction of the company. That is never a good situation. New investors usually insist on putting their representative on your Board to babysit their best interests, not yours. Set up your Board

so that you can add a new, friendly Director whenever the investors add one. Keep control.

- *Voting control.* Avoid all the complex share structures that can evolve into "special" features that give your investors enhanced voting rights, preferred shares, or onerous liquidation rights. Remember to make your corporate lawyer your new best friend. They can steer you clear of some of these traps.

- *Financial control.* Always try to time your fund-raising activities with your recent milestone accomplishments. Use them to increase your valuation and therefore you may give away less stock. Financial control also includes the check book. Be prepared to cosign every check that you issue. It will give you a chance to see every invoice and question those where you need to understand more about each expense. Like an auditor, pick out a few invoices at random and follow up on the details. Everyone will know that you are on top of your expenses.

- *IP control.* Make sure that your company's IP actually belongs to the company and not the individual employees who created it. This includes patent applications, trade secrets, and unique work processes. The worst-case scenario can happen when an employee leaves the company and takes some of your key IP with them. Remember that your best friend, your corporate lawyer, can ensure that all your IP is actually a corporate asset.

- *Operations control.* Today's startups can grow exponentially in a short time. You don't need to just be on top of this, you need to be in front of it. Too often large-scale company ramp-ups lead to a loss of their original core beliefs, focus, and goals. It's the founder's job to set the corporate goals and standards and to effectively and constantly communicate them to the entire team. It's a big task to keep everyone on the same page.

- *Shifting Your Role.* A lot is said about maintaining control of your company, but at some point, it is important to know when it is time to take the next step. That involves finding a high-level CEO to take over the day-to-day running of the company while you become the founder and board member. It will cost you shares. However, at that point in your company's growth pathway, it's better to own 5% of Megacorp than 90% of Minicorp.

My Real-Life Stories

Story #1

I was involved in a startup that became massively successful. We quickly expanded throughout North America and hired hundreds of employees. We grew so fast that we became a victim of own success.

Our rapid growth led to a watering down of our program's qualities and our corporate goals. This was not the fault of our employees. It was our inability to build the support systems for bringing on board a lot of new people in a short time.

The solution was simple but very expensive. We brought 400 employees from around the country into a convention center hotel complex. We socialized, told our company's story, ran three days of seminars, and got everyone singing off the same song sheet.

From that point forward, we established a strong human resources department that pioneered an employee indoctrination program and drove employee knowledge throughout the company. We regained operational control of our company.

Story #2

A company once tasked me to enhance their "customer-centric" focus. They regarded it as one of their strengths, and felt that over time, it was slipping away. Their management committee included the CEO, CFO, all their vice presidents and division managers. Some of them had never seen a customer. To them, they only existed as names on paper.

In order to turn this situation on its head, I tasked each committee member with becoming the "champion" of a specific customer. I delivered each executive a detailed account history, sales analysis, and contact list for their assigned customer. Not everyone was keen with this approach, but my message was very blunt, "If you really want to know what's happening out there, put your boots on and get your backside out there." It worked mostly and helped them restore the company's connection with its customers.

And If I Were You...

1. Do whatever it takes to keep control of your company during the critical early stages of development.
2. Find a good corporate lawyer and make them your very best friend. They can keep you ahead of the curve on share structure, option plans, Board makeup, shareholder voting, and everything else that you need to know. Think of them as your "legal survival and protect my interests manual."
3. Stage multiple financing events that coincide with your corporate performance milestones to reduce your team's dilution. You will keep control your company.
4. Own all your core IP.
5. Create a human resources role to train employees and maintain corporate standards.
6. Make sure that a majority of your Board of Directors share and support your vision.
7. Be the control person. Everybody needs to understand who's driving the bus.

CHAPTER 13

Dealmaking in Your Favor

Become the "Dealmaker in Residence"

Premise

Somehow dealmaking has acquired a spiritual mystique that is now commonly referred to as an "art." Nothing could be further from reality. Dealmaking is more of a *rubber meets the road* thing than an artform.

Conventional Thinking

Everyone who leads a young company evolves into a salesperson. You need to become the *Dealmaker in Residence* in order to attract and acquire good people, key suppliers, investors and, most importantly, customers.

There are so many different opinions on dealmaking, and so much has been written on it that it has become a blur. Dealmaking is a simple skill that is based on focus and hard work. In fact, we all do it, everyday. "*Who is going to drop the kids off at soccer, pick up the laundry or order dinner*"? We are constantly making some kind of deal.

Dealmaking really works when both parties get what they need, not necessarily what they want. The best deals are when everyone believes that they got a win. It's a world of compromise.

Always start out the negotiating process by defining what you want, and figure out how you might achieve it. Here are some real-world strategies for dealmaking with customers.

- Do your homework. Learn as much as you can about each customer before you ever meet with them. Read their public reports or news releases. Visit their plants. Talk to their customers. Knowledge is power when it comes to negotiating.

- Be seen as reasonable. It will cause others to be likewise and will accelerate the dealmaking process.
- Use personal issues to establish a common ground. I once negotiated with a CEO who was also a director of a national go-karting association, so I bought a go-kart before we met. When we did meet in his office, it was wall to wall go-kart paraphernalia and I had the opportunity to tell him that I owned one too. Instant common ground. I got the deal done and then sadly sold my go-kart.
- Understand the other person's needs. What is motivating them to deal with you? Is it increased revenue or replacing an outdated system? Are they number two in their industry and wanting to be number one? Any of these will shape their view of a deal. The more you know about the other side, the better you can position your offering.
- You don't need to destroy the other party. You need to get the deal that works for you, and if it works for both parties, it's a good deal. Keep it win–win.
- Take your competition out of the deal as quickly as possible. Don't let the other party perceive your competitors as a viable alternative for them. Cast them as too slow, too old school, too whatever, as long as they are relegated to a poor second choice.
- Understand the possibility of not reaching a deal. Part of deal-making is standing your ground and not reaching agreement. The only thing worse than walking away from a bad deal is doing one that can haunt you for years.
- Don't let others frame the negotiating timeline. I once negotiated with a group that was very interested in what time my flight home was leaving. They clearly wanted to squeeze my time, thinking that they would get a better last-minute deal. I simply told them that my wife was flying in that night and I would be in town for a week. A total fabrication, but it was worth the look on their faces.
- Have a plan B. While you always go into negotiations thinking that a deal will happen, it might not. Your negotiating

position is stronger if you have a clear strategy for a plan B. You don't need to share it with the other party. I never did, but I always looked two moves ahead and knew what to do next if the current deal didn't happen.

International dealmaking brings a whole unique set of elements to dealmaking. As you can imagine, negotiating in China is very different from doing a deal in South Africa. There is no substitute for having local knowledge and the best way to get it is through a local coach who can advise you on foreign customs and a law firm that has an office in whichever foreign country you are dealing with.

So often in life, it's the little things that can be a big deal. In one instance, I knew that my international hosts were taking me out to a fine restaurant, so I memorized how to order a meal in their language. My dinner hosts were mega impressed. Showing respect is always a winning strategy.

My Real-Life Story

Story #1

One of my major customers had a division that they wanted me to visit. Their plan was that I would convince this rogue division to join our corporate program. This was a classic example of me not doing my homework and it quickly became a suicide mission. There was a good reason that this rogue division was the only group in the company that didn't run our program. They simply hated everything that was supported by their head office and now that included me. I arrived at the meeting with my happy face on, but that didn't last very long. The theme of this meeting, as set by them, was "no, no and hell no." Meeting over! I packed my bags and fled town.

Story #2

What I initially thought would be a smooth dealmaking process turned into a messy event. Our two companies were a perfect fit for each other and we simply had to work out the details. What I thought was a common-sense presentation didn't make any inroads with them. The challenge here was that their new CEO, who was leading these negotiations, had no business experience and had just recently inherited the company after the sudden death of the founder. He didn't really understand the fundamentals of his own business and certainly not mine.

Fortunately, I had done my homework on this situation and was ready for it. I switched the focus of our conversation to how the addition of my service would increase the value of their company and polish its image with potential buyers. We immediately discovered our common ground and the deal got done.

And If I Were You...

1. Do your homework on every potential customer and understand what issues are most important to them.
2. Establish a common ground between the negotiating parties, the more personal the better. People want to do business with those that they can relate with.
3. Subtly frame your competition as an inferior second choice for anybody.
4. The best Plan A is a good Plan B.
5. Always be ready to walk away from a deal.
6. The dealmaking dumpster is full of bullies that overestimated their personal value, made greed their calling card, and inevitably failed because they couldn't structure win–win deals. Do better.

Selling Into Humungous Markets

Premise

Every day the world gets smaller, and it gets easier for young companies to sell into enticingly big international (and national) markets.

Conventional Thinking

Doing big deals is everyone's goal. It is an endorsement of your success. Selling into big markets, especially international ones, is a big status event and can be very profitable. Sometimes (but not always).

Big companies understand the potential problems associated with selling into international markets where risks can include fluctuating foreign currencies, shipping labilities, foreign legal and cultural issues, and third world ethical standards. All these variables need to be preidentified and built into the terms of any international sales deal, and most big companies are good at it.

This can be a different experience for young companies that may not fully understand or be attuned to the international subtleties of these deals. Everyone, regardless of the size of your company, needs to keep repeating this mantra, *"How do I get paid?"* Here are some of the things that young companies need to consider:

Domestic Markets. The draw to do big deals into international markets is always exciting, but before you take this leap, don't overlook the domestic markets that you can tap. In the United States alone, there are approximately 50 marketing areas with populations over one million people. That's a lot of market opportunity, and it is a lot less risky than any overseas deal.

The G20 Countries. Like the United States, the G20 countries, for the most part, have well-established banking systems and legal systems that are both understandable and workable (I would exclude Russia from this list). Your first international deal should really be in a most user-friendly place. Mine was in Toronto, Canada, simply because it is a big market right next door, and with an integrated banking network and no language issues. Any G20 country (well, actually G19 excluding Russia) is an easy baby step into international sales, and very low risk.

Developing Countries. Outside of the G20, there are a number of countries that have solid economies and may want to do business with you. The risk of dealing in these countries increases exponentially. In all my years, I never searched for customers in these types of countries, and they were never on my to do list. When I did get inquiries from these countries, I would treat them as one-time cash deals. I'd supply them, but only if I was paid up front, and I never expected a second order. This approach may seem harsh, but it protected my company.

China. Everyone would like to sell into China. It's a huge market with a multitude of different provinces, each with different regional governments and red tape, needs, tastes, and levels of sophistication. It is also an anomaly of known and unknown risks, not the least of which is a flexible approach to your IP rights. My experience in doing business in China was like going back to the good old days in the Wild West, sort of like gun fights at the OK Corral in Tombstone, Arizona. However, the appeal of doing business in China is irresistible. I know I've done both buy and sell deals there and it is a big rush but never forget how sketchy it can be.

I once was directed by a component supplier to deliver $10,000 in cash to their plant in order to secure my purchase. I delivered a brief case with the cash and a bottle of scotch whiskey and my order was delivered the next day. Interesting place!

Get paid up front, before your product leaves these shores, or prior to delivering anything. If you need to go to court with your client in China, forget it. You have lost. Chinese courts protect their citizens, and even if you are in the right, you are fighting a futile battle.

The Big Order. Beware of the *big order*, whether domestic or international. The big order that you have always dreamed about can be loaded with daunting risk. I have seen companies overreach their financial and operational limits in order to land and deliver on the big order, so much so that they put the very existence of their company on the line. Consider the mega customer that delays payment on the big order that you had already produced or delivered. This is a sure way to a cash flow disaster. Ten smaller deals are better than the dream deal that becomes a nightmare.

Getting Paid. For small companies, it doesn't matter if your big deal is international, domestic or with your brother-in-law. Your number one concern should be getting paid, on time and in full. Everything else is number two. Deals, as in life, often start out great. They start with the honeymoon, possibly followed by a not so great time and finally the divorce. Always make sure that your company is protected against these unexpected cash interruptions.

My Real-Life Story

I got a great lesson in how to concentrate on domestic markets from a telecom reseller that provided services throughout the country. They were becoming highly successful and I wanted to piggyback my systems on their network.

I met their founders and toured their facility in New York. It was very impressive, and I wanted to hear more about their expansion plans, specifically where they were establishing new network centers.

It turned out that their expansion plans were based on the National Football League (NFL). Never mind government statics, Designated Marketing Area analysis or television ownership models. They adopted a much more creative method. Their thinking was, if was good enough for the NFL to have a franchise based in a certain city, it was good enough for them. I had never heard this before and it cracked me up. When you really think about it, it actually makes sense. They piggybacked on the NFL's analysis of markets.

The craziness didn't stop there. While I was touring their network facility, I couldn't help but notice that they had great security, and the existing walls of their network rooms were three feet thick. The buildings that they were leasing were actually designed to withstand nuclear bomb attacks. They were buildings decommissioned by the federal government and repurposed as ideal computer centers. You can't make this stuff up.

It just goes to show you that there are lots of domestic opportunities out there, and some of them are even bomb proof.

And If I Were You...

1. Young companies need to put the brakes on jumping into international markets too soon.
2. Establish a solid cash flow from domestic markets before you ever consider international sales.
3. With every deal, keep repeating "*how do I get paid?*"
4. Beware of a single big order that can over stress you financially. Stage the big order into a series of smaller orders and get paid for each one as you go.
5. Pick a safe, friendly location for your first international sale. It will be a learning experience for your next deals.

CHAPTER 14

Communications, Networking, and Playacting

Becoming the Company Showman

The Premise

Your elevator pitch needs teeth and needs to be delivered by a "frontman." My favorite pitch was "Nobody Shoots Santa Claus."

Conventional Thinking

Elevator pitches have always been a vehicle for cold-call introductions such as at networking sessions, conferences, trade shows, and social gatherings. They serve a critical purpose in introducing yourself and your company.

However, in today's ultrafast-paced business environment where introductions have become analogous to speed dating, the elevator pitch has taken on new importance. Further, with social media's influence growing exponentially, and the inherently short attention span of visitors to your website, last estimated at six to eight seconds, the significance of a well-tailored, impactful elevator pitch cannot be overstated.

The issue is that most pitches go nowhere. If there is no interest or future action resulting from your pitch, they are dead-end efforts. That does not have to be the case at all.

The structure of the pitch is pretty well documented. Even within the 24 million responses that a Google search delivers, there is a commonality to the structure.

- *Who are you?*
- *What does your company do?*
- *What is the value proposition?*
- *Grab their attention*

Who you are and what your company does won't win you any major brownie points. The pitch should be brief. Its only role is for the other party to continue listening, with a modicum of interest or curiosity. The value proposition is where you score.

In my elevator pitch, I always zeroed in on the value proposition, namely, what can my company deliver in light of what the other party may respond to, always keeping in mind the other party's "hot buttons."

- *Can you enhance my profits or reduce my expenses?*
- *Will your services or products deliver results I can be proud of, or earn me bragging rights?*
- *Will this make me look good to my superiors, or my Board?*
- *Will it increase my bonus?*
- *Can you free up my time so I can focus on what I do best?*

The attention grabber is your last chance to deliver the knock-out punch. It should not simply be an invitation to visit your website (which they likely will not) or to hand out your business card or literature (which will find a home in the recycling bin). It needs to be proactive and actionable.

In my consulting practice, I offered access to government grants and strategies to enhance the client's margins and bottom line. In most instances, my attention grabber was "You know, nobody shoots Santa Claus. Let's meet next xx and I'll show you what I can do for you."

What's your elevator pitch?

My Real-Life Story

At one particular investor conference in China, I was invited to deliver a presentation on the opportunities available in my part of the world. With an expected audience of 3,000, I wanted to make sure my pitch was focused and effective.

After speaking with a number of associates, I confirmed that the "hot button" that was attracting these Asian investment groups to the conference, was "greed," that is, profit on investments. Security of investments was also an issue but well overshadowed by the love of outrageous financial returns.

Once I quickly established my credibility and position, I launched into the opportunity for profit-taking in a virtually untapped market. I cited examples that many of the investors present were envious of. I confirmed the surety of their funds in a stable political environment. Then, without hesitation, I was back on track promoting the profit factor. Over and over again, unabashedly.

For my attention grabber, I invited attendees to meet with me the next day, inferring that both my time at the conference and the availability of the best investment opportunities were "first come, first served." I was inundated with interest, and, in fact, had meetings virtually right through the night as well.

In another instance, I was scheduled to attend a Chamber of Commerce networking session. I knew which attendees I wanted to meet and court, but, in this stodgy crowd, I wanted to try to stand apart and be noticed.

I arrive late and intentionally sauntered in. I was dressed more casually than most attendees. As I wandered through the hall, I purposely did not immediately join any "friend-only clusters" and I avoided those where the group was comprised of people from the same company, or close business acquaintances. I had no interest in these closed "hen" parties.

I eventually joined the group that included my "target." I had my well-rehearsed pitch down pat. And, I never handed out a business card unless I was asked for one. My aura of independence and my being slightly offbeat was construed as "successful." It worked for me, and, in fact, still does.

And If I Were You...

1. Before you meet with a client, find out everything you can about them and prepare your pitch to reflect their needs. Industry, trade magazine, and Web research may provide a glimpse as to what interest you can instigate.

2. Communication is of paramount importance. For many people, it is a learned skill. Take sales acting classes to develop your networking persona.

3. Prior to attending a conference, trade show, or networking session, find out who the prospective attendees are and zero in on the ones you want to single out.

4. Stand apart. Be a bit of a business rebel. Don't simply fit in with everyone else flitting about your prospective lead at an event.

5. Don't improvise. Be prepared, and that includes practicing your elevator pitch where you can be provided with feedback.

6. If you are uncertain, test out your pitch with a client or contact whose business is not critical to you, or where the location is outside your immediate market area. If you mess up, the consequences will be minimal.

7. Be proactive in your elevator pitch. Be animated. Don't just recite the "party line" pitch.

Delivering Compelling Presentations

Premise

Pitching your case to investors, partners, or potential customers is part of business. It demands that you put on your Prada groveler kneepads, fix a (real or illusory) conqueror's confidence-exuding smile on your face, and enter the office or boardroom of judgment.

Conventional Wisdom

Most of what is taught about presenting, or written about, or encapsulated in training videos and social media tidbits is incomplete. It's not false, mind you, just woefully inadequate. Only experience from those who have faced the firestorm can offer strategies that have been proven successful in pitching an idea, product, or service.

To the uninitiated, the prospect of delivering a presentation can be intimidating. But it doesn't need to be. By utilizing a number of sensible and readily implementable tactics, your delivery can spell the difference between "no thank you" and "let's do it." Here are the key techniques.

Your *appearance* is the first thing your audience sees. Dress appropriately to match the group you are presenting to. Be it formal or casual, try to blend in. I remember one incident when a developer was presenting his tourism project to a remote township audience. He sent his best "big city" planners to meet the community and instructed them accordingly to dress casually. They did. However, their casual clothes were right out of the packaging. The shirts and pants still had all the new-clothes crease (press) lines, and this was not lost on the locals. They felt that they were being patronized and the development permit was turned down. That's all it took.

Maintain *eye contact* and look for those in your audience who seem to be agreeing with your pitch, or responding in a positive manner. Build allies.

Don't distribute *written material* before you present. The audience will get distracted while you are trying to keep their attention. Instead, hand out your material when you are winding up, or before people leave. It gives your audience the opportunity to revisit your presentation after it is completed.

Your *attitude* conveys your confidence in who you are, what you are presenting, and what you are asking for. Maintain a sense of decorum, but not standoffishness. Use *body language* to your advantage. If you are jittery, then hide it as best you can.

I have always felt that maintaining a good *sense of humor* is an effective ice breaker that calms you and lowers the defenses of your assemblage. Humor transcends barriers.

Keep your *message simple*. You have a presentation for a purpose, a specific "ask." Make sure your audience understands the purpose of your presence there, and what you need from them. To that end, always remember what's in it for them. Human nature makes people genuinely selfish and that hunger needs to be addressed.

The *four "hot buttons"* that trigger reactions from people are *greed*, *ego*, *pride*, and *sloth*. Make sure your presentation manages to hit one or more of these coveted behavioral hot buttons with the intended decision makers.

- *Greed—What can I personally get out of this?*
- *Ego—Will this make me look good to others in the company, my associates, the community?*

- *Pride—If I go along with the "ask," will this give me "bragging rights"?*
- *Sloth—Will this make my job easier? Will this lower my workload and give me more free time?*

If you are using *PowerPoint*, keep the verbiage simple. The text should be talking points for you, and not the full-blown content of your Business Plan. Nothing is worse than a slide with a ton of writing that your audience is busy trying to read as you are speaking. You do not want to draw attention from yourself.

The *time you will have to present* will be predetermined. Make sure your presentation does not have to be hurried to complete within the limited timeframe. Pace yourself. Practice and time it in advance of the event.

Tell stories. People love stories, especially if you are relaying personal or business experiences that relate directly to your presentation.

Don't oversell. At some point, you will be able to see when your audience has achieved some "buy-in" with you. At that point, stop selling and instead work to solidify your position. You may actually become one with your audience, and sensing that, you will have succeeded.

Presentations demand you carrying out your role as the spokesperson for your company or organization. That implies maintaining an image, an appearance, and a character. It is a performance. You may be comfortable assuming this role. However, many are not. It can be a learned skill and a confidence builder.

Giving a presentation is analogous to being on stage. Take improvisation classes that encourage you to step outside your comfort zone and take on roles that help you deliver effective presentations.

My Real-Life Story

Delivering presentations in a foreign environment is difficult, especially if you are working with a translator. There is a time delay while you wait for translations, and you are never 100% certain that what you are saying is being properly translated.

I found myself floundering during an investment presentation in China. Regardless of what I said, the small audience around the

Boardroom was not reacting, and I had little confidence in the translator assigned to me. I had a second presentation opportunity in two days, and I was determined to do better.

I contacted my embassy and got the name of a professional who could help me properly package my message in the style that my audience would be comfortable with.

Together, we redid my PowerPoint and loaded it with photos and graphics, including paying homage to my host audience as a sign of respect.

I dismissed my previous translator and hired the pro who helped me with my presentation. Not only was she more competent than the previous person but she was also far more presentable.

My second presentation was specifically packaged for my audience, and it was a success. It taught me that it was more important that my audience hear what they need to hear instead of me trying to deliver what I want them to hear. This is a fine, but important distinction.

And If I Were You...

1. Be flexible. Know everything about your audience before you present and build your presentation around what they might need to hear, more than about what your pitch is.
2. Practice, practice, practice. This will help you refine your content and timing.
3. Maintain eye contact, talk slowly, and change up the pace of your presentation often.
4. Take your cues from your audience and learn to react to those cues. That may necessitate changing your pace, or interjecting stories of your personal experiences, or humor. All are effective tools in bringing your audience back from the abyss.

Lights, Camera: The Spotlight's on You

The Premise

Theatrics is your key to greater, more effective communications, and writing more business.

Conventional Wisdom

The assumption is that we communicate when we speak, as well as when we carry out group meetings. We feel that we actually reach out and convey what we had intended to get across. That's likely only partially true, and way oversimplistic.

For most of us, we may think that our well-organized pitch, our networking interaction at a trade show or conference, or our graphically stunning presentation at an investor dog-and-pony show, has hit home. Hold off on that victory lap, please. In truth, there are many other dynamics at work here.

Theatrics are the key to developing highly effective communications skills including the spoken word, body language, nonverbal clues, personal interaction, and your very presence on the business stage. The disciplines of live theater can hone your ability to score every time you bank on a positive response from your listeners, be that a single client or a massive gathering.

The doctrines of a live theater performance are so useful. Understanding what drives actors, or even students of theater is immensely important and readily transferable into the business milieu, so much so that business schools such as Duke University and Stanford are including improv into their curriculum to help future leaders cope in virtually every situation they may find themselves in.

Improv is theater's training ground that teaches participants how to respond to any situation quickly, feed off the others' dynamics, be fearless, skate when presented with the unknown and unexpected, and, most importantly, communicate effectively enough to draw an intended reaction from those around you.

We all need to recognize that we are all just players on a stage, where communication, or acting, is simply taken for granted. It should not be. Understand that business is people. It's not so much about you as it is about your intended audience. Voice, projection, attitude, stance, movement, body language are all the tools that theatrics can teach you and your people. It is a skillset that can be taught through improv.

Imagine how astonishing that could be for you. The amount of control you could exert would be colossal. Welcome to theater, theatrics, and improv.

Here are a few theatric lessons that apply to business. The analogies abound.

- Theater forces you to step into the spotlight and expand your comfort zone.
- In business, investors look for that "beyond everyday mundane" edge. Acting encourages you to do things beyond the everyday.
- Actors encounter failure but necessarily bounce back for their next performance.
- Selling is like acting auditions every day.
- Actors exemplify showmanship, like a businessperson relating a story.
- Critical situations in business temporarily suspend our safety nets, as does acting.
- Acting forces empathy, understanding, and dealing with others' needs, and seeing others' experiences through their lens.
- Listening and reacting to others is so crucial in business. You learn to take cues from the others "on stage" or from around the boardroom table.
- Improv is about collaboration rather than competition. You look good by making others look good. That is a sound business practice as well.

My Real-Life Story

This is a classic "read and react" story as only my experience, and my having been put on the spot can recap.

There was an occasion that my partner and I were invited to present to a large group of high-level managers and their support teams. It was an excellent opportunity for my company. And we were prepared with a first-class PowerPoint and handout package. The works.

It was somewhat of an uncomfortable situation for me for two reasons. Firstly, I had recently launched my company and we really needed a customer. Secondly, I felt that, in that environment in which we found ourselves, we were fighting above our weight class. These people, and the power they wielded, were intimidating.

My partner took the lead in the presentation, and, in his usual slick style, was busily selling our firm to the group. This was his one-and-only delivery style, regardless of the audience. However, with this group, they did not care. That was not why they were assembled there.

My experience kicked in. Watching the body language, the lack of connection with the group, I knew we were losing the audience.

I stepped in, ever so carefully, and took over the show. I discarded our dog-and-pony PowerPoint and, instead, opened the event for discussion. I paced away from the podium and toward the group. I needed to hear exactly what their expectations were so that I could respond accordingly. Suddenly, I had their attention. My partner had focused on us, while I zeroed in on the attendees, and that was appreciated.

Body language and dress spoke of a casual professionalism, and I matched them by doffing my suit jacket and tie, and rolling up my sleeves. I was becoming one of them.

I found an opportunity to relay the story of how we had started our company on the back of a napkin while sitting at a local diner. I did this knowing full well that the client also had humble beginnings. This made them simpatico to our struggles.

The meeting from thereon went well. It ended with a "call to action" on my part, and their request for a proposal from my company to be presented and discussed at a meeting date that was arranged before we left.

I realized afterwards that it was the lessons learned in improv that complimented my natural instincts. I now had my communications business model which I have since adhered to throughout my career.

And If I Were You...

1. Hire a sales coach with some acting experience. Make sure they understand your business and the situations you generally find yourself in.

2. Take improv classes for yourself and your team. They are not only fun, but you will learn critical communication strategies and techniques that you will find yourself applying in business. You will also learn more about your own team.

3. Test yourself, and others, in mockup situations where the unexpected is the norm.

4. Develop storytelling skills, described in another important skillset. People love stories and relate well to them. Create stories about yourself and the origins of your business, and feel free to harmlessly embellish them sufficiently to generate interest, empathy, and attention.

5. As in acting, learn to put yourself in others' shoes, namely, your audience at hand. If these are outside your normal comfort zone, try harder.

6. Practice, practice, practice. Develop your own style, one that is comfortable for you. It needs to become second nature.

CHAPTER 15

Business Is a Game Best Played to Win

Playing on the Business Battlefield

The Premise

Business is more than a game. It's war.

Conventional Thinking

Quite often business is likened to a game, with its boardgame rules and strategies, and its end goal trophies and prizes. Chess, Monopoly, and Risk are prime examples, encompassing clashing teams, or real estate one-upmanship ("one-upwomanship"?) or even world domination. In the grand scheme of things, that thinking is child's play compared to the real world of business.

Commonplace comparisons between business and sports are somewhat more appropriate. Business and sports share commonality.

- *Coaches are the leaders.*
- *Team names, uniforms, and logos are the brands.*
- *Key players most often elevated to worship status, are the endorsements.*
- *Rules are, well, the rules to abide by, or pay the penalty, but they also get bent.*
- *Scoring is celebrated.*

- *Winning is everything (despite what the losers might say about giving it their best).*
- *It's often a team effort, with tons of strategizing and second guessing.*
- *The gameplan itself is the business plan.*

However, as often as these correlations are cited, they are harmless. Nobody gets wounded or dies. Everyone lives to play another day, and opponents often share some comradery, celebrate past encounters, and boast about winning "the next one."

These are all distractions and any analogies are dangerously oversimplistic. Business is not a boardgame, or an afternoon game of "capture the flag." Business has much higher stakes. It is all-out war.

- *The market supports infinite players that can coexist but only a finite number can achieve domination, and that is what leader entrepreneurs strive for.*
- *There are risks, landmines, and elastic ethics that continually shift what is acceptable, and what is several strides beyond conformity.*
- *Theft of products (i.e., reverse engineering) and plundering competitors' key people are commonplace.*
- *Acquiring gray market data and lists is frowned upon, but just so.*
- *There are few coincidences. End runs designed to disrupt are prevalent. Weren't Apple's iPhones introduced just ahead of Samsung's phone devices, or vice versa?*
- *And most importantly, the survival of the fittest is universal. The weak die out, the strongest mount the pedestal of victory and recognition, at least, for a while, anyways.*

Business is all-out war, and the battle tactics often cited from Sun Tzu's *The Art of War* provide valuable lessons and strategies for the entrepreneur. The following represent Tzu's teachings remodeled to apply to the business world.

- Winning is fine; in fact, it is expected, but do not rest on your laurels. The next battle is just around the corner.

- Expand your horizon to take in the entire battlefield. Look at the big picture. Adopt the "spectator mode," analogous to seeing the playing field from high up in the stands of a stadium.
- Invest in your people. The market may only see your product or service, but your team got you to where you are today or where you are heading to tomorrow.
- Be an effective leader, with a clear vision of where you want to be, and a pathway to get you there.
- Prepare for victory, but it is always prudent to have a Plan "B," just in case.
- The best business battle is the one you avoided because you had already successfully out-maneuvered your competition.
- In any negotiations, always try to leave something on the table. Winning is fine. Total defeat of the competitors negates the opportunity for future collaboration.
- Everything that happens reflects someone's motivation in making it happen. Understand that before you react.
- Try to capture market share without destroying the market with, for example, price wars and lost leader events, or nobody wins. Your industry as a whole loses.
- Maximize business intelligence. That includes understanding your own company's strengths and capabilities, but also know your competitors as well.
- Learn to play nice. It opens doors.
- Strategic partnerships, licensing, and acquisitions create almost instant growth for your firm and are far more cost-effective than paralleling growth via in-house efforts.

My Real-Life Story

I had a client who, by the time I got involved, was already on a downward spiral. They had lost significant market share and their old-school owners were reluctant to change their products or strategies. "Things will change" was the rallying cry, and they did. They just kept seeing more red ink.

What I did was create a "war room" and convinced them to hire a younger, successful industry player who had proven that he was a leader and an innovator.

I then created a research team that was commissioned to research every aspect of where the industry was heading, including technology and upcoming developments, as well as carrying out a comprehensive survey of what the customers wanted and needed. The client base was to drive the direction of the business, which, to my surprise, was actually a novel approach for the ownership.

There was also a housecleaning carried out among the managers and senior staff, primarily those who gave no credence to suggestions and recommendations made by the company's employees and field operatives who were actually doing the day-to-day work, including customer service and liaison. They knew what the issues and challenges were but were being ignored. That was not acceptable.

Eventually, the business turned about. It was a painful process, but the core business was worth salvaging. As I understand it, they are still around today and considered one of the industry's progressive players.

Think of business as a war. I have attempted to present a blueprint of strategies as shown earlier that are highly applicable to you running your business. Please consider adopting as many as you can. They will make a difference to your entrepreneurial or management success.

And If I Were You...

1. Never assume business is just a game. While there are likenesses, business plays for keeps.
2. Don't assume that others will play by your standards, or by generally accepted rules and standards. Many won't, so don't set yourself up for unexpected intrusions from competitors.
3. Things change. Markets, technology, competitors, the economy, customers, demographic bases, trends, fads, tastes, client needs, and even threats beyond your ability to influence, such as pandemics, war, and government policies. Stay on top of as much as you can, and develop mitigating strategies for everything under, or out of, your control.
4. Create a "war room" with your best and brightest. Listen to what they tell you.

Business No-No's: Avoid Doing Any of These

The Premise

Business no-no's. Here's what you should *not* do in business.

Conventional Thinking

There is no dire shortage of business "how to" books, courses and consultants dealing with how to plan, market, brand, beg for money, build a team, motivate, hire, reprimand, fire, provide good customer service, and a host of other strategies to make you as successful as you can possibly be. They all have merit.

However, there are far too few tidbits of advice on what *not* to do, that is, the kind of behavior that will cost you, sometimes a little, and often a lot.

As you review the "no-no's" below, you would think that common sense would dictate that, quite logically, these need to be avoided, and that your "stranger danger" alert would go off. But human behavior is often an irrational beast.

You may find yourself slipping into any of these behavioral patterns, subconsciously, or be wondering, in hindsight, if you made some sort of error in judgment and how best to rewrite history.

The best strategy is to be keenly aware of these business faux-pas ahead of time, and try not to step into the snare. So, here we go with the *"Don't Do These."* They are not presented in any order of priority. Just assume they are all degrees of bad.

- Don't stalk your customer. Once you submit a quote or presentation, the temptation is to stay on top of it, which is fine. Smothering is bad. If a client feels your ever-presence, they will likely walk away. The solution is to stay in touch with the client with a certain degree of frequency, but never looming or smothering, but just hovering.
- Never trust a person who lets you down twice. Once is forgivable. We are all human. Twice is not a coincidence. Say goodbye, regardless of what empty promises they make to you.

- If you are digging yourself into a hole, stop digging! This applies to any situation you find yourself. Digging deeper as part of any salvage strategy is self-defeating. All you get is a deeper hole that gets tougher or impossible to claw your way out of.

- Don't believe third hand information. Communication is often a game of "broken telephone." It's actually a popular children's party game and belongs there alone. What you hear from your third (or fourth, or fifth) level source will not resemble what was originally said. I had a partner who relayed feedback from clients that sent me into a tailspin until I started checking back with the source. More often than not, my partners penchant for exaggeration colored the information he passed along to me.

- Never complain to a client. They don't care. They may show some empathy, but it's more so impatience to get on with the meeting. It also weakens your position and image. Trust me, nobody wants to hear about your flu, stock market losses, car accident, or issues with your wife or kids. People have their own baggage to deal with.

- The little person on your shoulder is warning you. It takes maturity to listen to it.

- Try not to give up control of your company. It's great to have investors or partners, but if that means foregoing the ability to govern, then you basically become an equity-holding employee. You have given up your brainchild.

- In the same vein, avoid "vulture capital" investors who insist on including a ratchet clause in any deal, the implication of which, means that as you fall short in your stated performance, they take more of your shares. No deal is worth that kind of Sword of Damocles over your head.

- Don't do things you are not really good at. You can always find a way to farm out activities that eat up your time, don't deliver revenues, or require too much of a learning curve. Just do what you like and what you are good at. Chances are they go hand in hand.

- Never stop learning and growing. Whether it be upcoming industry trends, new competitors on the horizon, technology enhancements, or anything that can impact your business, make sure you attend those boring conferences and trade shows. Participate in trade associations and remain ever-vigilant. Don't stagnate.
- Don't blame others in your company when things go wrong. You hired them. You trained them. Be big enough to bite the bullet. Clients will respect that too.
- Maintain a watchful eye on your competitors, but don't obsess about them. Stay on track and let them lose sleep about you instead.
- Assume things change over time. Whether your business or industry is going through great or horrible times, that will likely change. Hang in there and save enough money for a rainy day.
- As a corollary to items highlighted above, when things are slow and you are cutting expenses, contrary to what people are telling you, marketing is the last activity to cut back. In fact, you should be spending even more. Remember, marketing drives sales, which delivers cash flow.
- Spread your client base around. Selling a high percentage of your products or services to one client is great in good times, and suicide if they decide to renegotiate or slow themselves down. The insurance industry has learned their lesson. On large coverage they write "subscription policies," where any number of insurers band together, each covering a percentage of the risk. So, spread your risk around.
- Don't think so highly of yourself that people crane their necks looking up at you on your pedestal. Nobody likes that.

There are undoubtedly more don'ts, but if you understand and appreciate the ones cited herein, then your own protective instincts, namely your common sense, will begin to govern your decision-making process, and you will install inhibitors on anything that can harm you, or your company.

My Real-Life Story

I had a partner in one of my businesses. I had entered the partnership with the best of intentions and expectations, which, I assumed, he did too.

Things were fine for a while. His business ideas were sometimes grandiose, but since I maintained the controlling shares in the business, I was able to hold him in check. Besides that, we had an almost-working relationship in which I did most of the work while he did most of the dreaming.

I began to see changes in him. He became more loudly outspoken, complaining, and easily angered. His boisterous persona scared several of our clients away, and I was not far behind.

I tried speaking with him, but the inevitable outcome was a catfight. I retreated, assuming, quite wrongly, that the situation would settle out. The hole I was digging got deeper.

Drugs became his issue, going from the occasional joint to hallucinogens. He stole from the company. His wife left him, and he spiraled downward but still I was reluctant to deal with this.

In the end, the situation became unbearable, and almost impossible to salvage. It cost me a fair amount of money, including legal fees to send him on his way to wreak havoc on others.

I was savaged, but retribution was not far away. He approached one of my competitors, one whom I had no love for. Their CEO called me to ask about my ex-partner. It was cruel of me to speak kindly of him. I barely felt any remorse. They deserved each other.

The *don't* list mentioned previously provides a host of actionable items. Read them carefully and determine if any, apply to you. If so, work on it.

And If I Were You...

1. Always think before you act or jump. Everything has consequences.
2. Trust your gut instinct. It got you where you are today.
3. You have a "fear or flight" protective intuition. Pay attention. It is designed to protect you.
4. You need to see yourself as your number one priority. If there is anything that has the potential to harm you, deal with it quickly. The pain will go away faster.

CHAPTER 16

Creating Value and Net Worth

Weaponize Your Soft Assets to Cash Out

Premise

Pretty much every startup is perceived as a cash strapped *wanna-be*. You can alter this perception by creating a bundle of "soft" assets that don't appear on your balance sheet, but they will bring credibility and value to your company.

Conventional Thinking

Traditional thinking is that a company just naturally develops the so-called soft assets or value as it matures over time. In many cases they just automatically occur as part of doing business. Startups can do way better than this laissez faire approach. They can actually shape their own future.

Soft assets are unlike tangible or even intangible assets. You can't touch or feel them like inventory or equipment, but with a little creativity, you can craft them and make them work for you.

Startups can create soft value right out of the box; the earlier the better. Most of them are inexpensive to do, and they will dramatically enhance your status in your industry and increase your standing in the community.

In the end, these soft assets can greatly increase the real value of your enterprise. I always looked at how I could *weaponize* these to my advantage; you're going to do them anyway so why not shape them to punch up your story. These are some of my favorites.

Legal Stuff: When you are going to set up your new company, add on some bells and whistles. Things like a shareholder's agreement, an employee stock option plan and key employee contracts, will buff up your image and voila, you've just moved up in the corporate food chain.

Accounting: Get a name brand accounting firm. They are always looking for new clients and if they like your pitch, you can end up using their brand on your letterhead. It seems that every day some corporate executive goes to prison for monkeying around with the "books." A good accounting image will differentiate you from the bad guys.

Intellectual Property: Find something unique in your offering or product and file a patent application on it. Rename it and make IP part of your trade secrets. Make it part of your secret sauce while hiding it behind the curtain. It creates a mystique.

Data Rooms: Data rooms are usually associated with big companies when they are doing mergers or takeovers. Act like one the big guys from day one. Stick all your corporate documents, agreements, and financials into a file in the cloud and you become a big boy too. You're going to do this stuff anyway so why not organize it into one place and call it a "data room." Your investors will love it.

Team Strength: This is pure packaging. When you launch your new company, you are naturally going to surround yourself with good people with great credentials, including members of your Advisory Board. The packaging aspect here is to highlight all this experience and make it part of your brand.

Systems: It's a fact that most leaders of their respective business sectors have better internal systems than their competitors. A new enterprise is going to acquire new computers and software, so get the best and then brag about it. *We're better than them.*

Innovation and Novelty: Position yourself as new, better, disruptive, the future. When you're walking down the street and you see a dirty old penny on the ground, you keep on walking. If it was a shiny new penny, you would stop and pick it up. Everyone likes a shiny new penny. Be one.

Community Involvement: Community involvement is an honorable thing, but find the one that is the flavor of the day. That's the one that attracts the most media coverage, or the "must do thing" of the year. Attach your wagon to the "in" cause and smile for the cameras.

Brand Recognition: Create a brand image on day one. Use as many sensory elements as you can, whether they are based on cool technology, a flashy style or maybe romantic pictures in Venice. Creating this image will shape how people will form their first impression of you and your brand.

Corporate Image: Get a cool office located in a "*nouveau*" environment. That's usually in the "up and coming" part of town, which really means cheap leases. I once leased a space above a brew pub and worried that the big downtown glass tower lawyers, accountants, and venture capital guys wouldn't come to see me. I was totally wrong. They loved to visit the new trendy neighborhood and would always insist on a meeting just before lunch so we could hit the pub at noon. Best draw ever.

Online Presence: There is no better place to mold your image than your online presence. It's essential to push your story online. Launch a social presence the day you start your enterprise. Sell your idea and do a little video about your team, your goal, and why you are a game changer. Everyone checks out your online presence and more people will see this than you can ever meet face-to-face. Control your message.

Influencers: The world of online influencers is crazy. Most of them have incredible reach. I know one that has never done anything notable in his life and yet he has three million social media followers. His full-time job is to share the details of his life with his followers. My full-time job was to get him to say nice things about my new enterprise to three million people.

World Domination: Entrepreneurs in every developed country in the world are always on the hunt for next awesome product or service. I once demonstrated a new product in a major market and used that exposure to get some media coverage overseas. I was flooded with enquires and turned some of them into licensing deals that were like free money to me.

And my all-time favorite,

Create an Enemy: Make one up. It's human nature that everyone hates the enemy. Those are the guys in the black hats while you're wearing the white one. Define your competition as too old fashioned, too expensive, or too whatever, as long as they are the villains and you are the hero. Image, image, image.

My Real-Life Story

I once started a company where our clear end game was to sell it to one of the large players that were expanding into our business sector. We had lined up our funding and we were well on the way to achieving the customer acceptance that would make us a takeover target for the big guys. They regarded us as new, disruptive, and desirable.

Once the buyers were circling, we started to dream about the pot of gold at the end of the rainbow. With our payday near at hand, one of our advisers asked about the status of our "data room." Our what?

So, we scrambled to build a data room. It turns out that a data room is actually a mega file that includes everything that you have ever done—from the original doodle on a napkin to your corporate financials. This exercise seemed like a pain, but it actually turned out to be a big win.

The next step in the sale of the company was the easy part. We negotiated a price with one of the big guys and shook hands. Then the minions arrived. The minion army was made up of their lawyers and bean counters that were tasked to dot every "*i*" and cross every "*t*." We simply turned our data room over to them and they got everything they needed.

Deal done, we got the cash, happy ending!

And If I Were You...

1. Soft assets are more of an image thing than a balance sheet thing—figure out what works for your situation and milk it.
2. You are probably going to do soft value things as part of your company launch and growth. Shape them to polish your image and drive up your perceived value.
3. Use your soft assets as a way to differentiate yourself from all the others in your sector.
4. Don't wait. Set up a data room today. The earlier the better.
5. Data rooms are not the exclusive purview of big companies but are just as important to any company that is considering doing a major financing or an exit transaction.

CHAPTER 17

Exit Strategies

Getting Out With Money in Your Jeans

Build It to Sell It

The Premise

Build your business with the specific goal of selling it. That requires special attention to what areas you need to focus on as you start, grow, and operate your enterprise.

Conventional Thinking

We tend to think that the businesses we create are "forever," and it seems all the excitement, roadblocks, sweat equity, and challenges we endure in the process are meant to be critical fabrics interwoven into the venture that we, alone, brought to fruition. This business owes you longevity, right?

Well, get over it. The average life span of a business, according to a McKinsey study, is less than 18 years, down from 68 years in 1958. Other reports state that 10 years is the average lastingness of a business. Looking longer term, only 0.5% of all companies make it to 100 years.

This is not an occasion to wring your hands in consternation waiting for the doomsday clock to count down. It is an opportunity that many businesspeople see as an asset you nurture, grow, and sell, passing the baton onto other businesspeople or companies, while you enjoy the fruits of your labor, or take on another entrepreneurial challenge (possibly between Pina Coladas on the beach).

This is often deemed the business "cycle of life" and clearly demands that you design and plan your company for the purpose of divestiture at the right time, at an acceptable financial gain.

Another possible end-play alternative is succession, handing the reigns down to family members. Far too often, the next generation does not carry your entrepreneurial genes, or drive, or hands-on experience and training. The result is often not pretty.

Of the dozen or more business successions I have witnessed, one was hugely successful, but this scenario was dwarfed by so many others that floundered, and where the "kids" lost the keys to the shop, and their leased Porsches along with them.

If you agree with this line of "build it to sell it" thinking, then everything in your business model should be intentionally designed for sell-readiness.

- Don't make yourself indispensable. We often talk about "personal branding" and "championing," but, over time, that focus and attention needs to be shifted more so to the company brand, and less to you.
- Keep your business model as simple as possible. Simple is easier to sell.
- From the very onset, identify potential buyout corporate competitors or those businesses who could realize some advantage by acquiring you. Watch their acquisition goings-on so that you can understand their corporate strategy and see how you might fit in, fill their market or product gaps, or deliver some impetus to their plans for growth and diversification.
- In some instances, what you may have already designed or created is a "cog" that a larger company may only be in the process of development. It is likely cost and time-effective to simply buy you out. You can actually plan for that scenario.
- Think about your prime assets, what is valuable, or possibly invaluable. This could logically include any of the following.
  - Client lists
  - Ability to data mine your client base
  - Intellectual property, copyrights, or proprietary modeling or designs

- ° Lucrative agreements and licenses
- ° Your brands that have a high degree of market awareness
- ° Your team of the brightest and best. Human resources have great value.
- ° Your very business model that has proven successful

My Real-Life Story

Story #1

I have always considered myself a "startup junkie," but only now, in hindsight, do I realize that designing, launching, and building a business is the adrenaline that fuels me. The longer-term operational side has always had me searching for some new challenge or opportunity. As such, selling my businesses were and still are an inherent and integral component of my "business cycle of life."

In one of my businesses, I was approached by a group looking to do a secondary public market financing. They needed news and success stories to attract investors.

Our company had always sought out working relationships with highly recognizable multinationals and Fortune 500 firms. We were the kind of "news" that the buyers needed, and we all clearly recognized that. We used it to our advantage throughout our buyout negotiations.

Story #2

In designing, funding, and constructing a manufacturing plant that produced a specialized wood fiber product, I knew well in advance that my competitors were few and that several automobile parts and plastic compounding giants were always needing another source of supply. This relationship was carefully nurtured from the get-go and proved valuable downstream.

Story #3

Even closer to home is a Business Consulting Firm, which I founded years ago. I have purposely morphed the company focus from "me" to "us." I have generated proprietary business and economic modeling tools, and other IP. I know my competition, as well as companies that deliver services complimentary to my own. When my "run" is done, I will likely package this very business for sale. It would seem that I am heeding my own advice.

And If I Were You...

1. Protect both your hard and soft assets. They are valuable pieces in the business selling game.
2. Carefully determine where your business fits a niche in the marketplace primarily controlled by the "big boys," and how what you have, delivers value-added for them.
3. Control every major decision or direction in your business because you have a roadmap.
4. Build a close team that understands the play, and where their combined expertise and skill sets can help drive the strategic building process.
5. For anyone who helps you score, make sure you reward them well and let them know it beforehand. I always did and loyalty was never an issue.
6. Identify and track the companies that may be potential purchasers of your company.
7. Build your internal systems to allow a seamless acquisition for buyers.
8. Document everything as you grow. This will increase your value.
9. Maintain bullet-proof financial records. You will need them.
10. You must carefully consider what you want and expect from your business down the road, if you are a disciple of "build to sell." If you are, it takes a fair degree of foresight and planning in virtually every decision you make to be able to follow through on this objective, and profit from it.

When Enough Is Enough

Premise

It's time to seriously consider a change "when you're cursing a donkey, wishing it was a thoroughbred." That's the type of marker that tells you enough is enough.

Conventional Thinking

How do you know when it's time to say goodbye to your current business before you move on, retire, sell, or get swept up by that new exciting business adventure? It's rarely a black-and-white omen that flashes before your eyes. It's generally a feeling, a human instinct, a glimmer of a warning or a distraction, that provides the signal that change is, or should be imminent.

The first and foremost reason would be that your business is failing, possibly outpaced by competitors, lagging behind the market or technology, or just simply stagnating; too much effort demanded from you with too little rewards and financial or emotional returns. Business needs to be a two-way relationship, that is giving and getting.

You rarely just walk away. You have built something of value in your business model, possibly IP, and, of course, hard assets, inventory, and work-in-progress that you may have invested in. There are a number of exit strategies dealt with in detail in another chapter in this book. This chapter, however, is how to recognize that you need to seriously consider doing something different. How do you know?

- Certainly, an obvious reason for "enough" revolves around health or family issues. These tend to jump to the forefront, and, if not easily resolved, occupy your time, attention, and sense of priority. You might be ready to choose another path.
- You have simply reached your goals that you had set for yourself. Congratulations! That feeling of self-satisfaction quickly gives way to the need for a greater or different challenge.
- You recognize that something is wrong, and you seek out sounding boards like trusted business friends and associates, mentors, advisers, or a contracted business consultant. When you are disinterested in any gems of advice and feedback you get, you should know that your decision to pivot to another direction has already been taken, consciously or subconsciously. You have already left the building.
- Your business is your paramour, your sweetheart, your life distraction. But the honeymoon is over. Your interaction becomes tedious, boring, or simply unfulfilling. You feel trapped and maybe you are frustrated that you just don't have

the time to do some of other nonbusiness "fun things" that you hoped being an entrepreneur would provide. You are simply falling out of love.

- Perhaps you have reached your financial target and accumulating more wealth is not as high priority as when you were hungry.
- Another opportunity comes your way, and you realize that the excitement it generates for you is something that you once had for your existing venture but has since faded. Time to renew and go in another direction.
- Your people come to you with issues and problems that need your resolution skills and authority. It's not that you don't care, but you care less. Possibly even consider them an intrusion or annoyance.
- Your customers become an annoyance. You lose respect for them or vice versa. Complaints have increased. If you care, fix it. If you don't, move on, since the chances of further damaging your business and lowering its resale value becomes a concern.
- When you planned and started your business, you were eager to learn, expand your knowledge, and stay attuned to your prospective markets. Perhaps now, learning is less important to you. Your business will suffer from this complacency.
- You may have become sloth-like, taking your time to return e-mails and phone calls, late coming into the office. Jumping onto business leads has become a chore rather than an exciting opportunity.

There really are no shortages of planned or unplanned reasons or life events that may have placed less emphasis or focus on your business. None of that matters, other than the fact that it is having a detrimental influence on your livelihood. You need to deal with it, and that in itself, can represent a positive transition in your life. I sincerely hope so.

My Real-Life Story

I was commuting to a client, and this particular trip included a ferry ride, so I had time to relax and enjoy one of my favorite pastimes: people-watching.

This older gentleman, well in his seventies, walked by me, weathered briefcase in hand. His slightly slouched posture and rambling gait made the shoulders of his business suit appear oddly disheveled. His lined face and gray stubble gave him the appearance of someone unhappy being where he was. Perhaps it was my imagination, but he seemed crestfallen and cheerless.

He took his seat at a workstation adjacent to mine. Opening his case, he took out a stack of papers, a calculator, and his cellphone, which began to ring. Hands shaking slightly, he answered, and by the nature of the call, it became obvious he was working on some job cost or proposal.

It seemed incongruous. This guy should not have been hustling for business. It was not right. He deserved better at his age. That very day I made myself a promise not to be like him. I would better prepare myself for when "enough is enough."

The experienced entrepreneur has the ability to plan their business life carefully and better prepare for exiting their business in an orchestrated fashion that provides them with the resources and the freedom of lifestyle choices when they are ready.

And If I Were You...

1. Never just walk away from your business. There is usually a financial gain to be realized from your hard work and entrepreneurial initiative.

2. Listen to your body. Your health is a great barometer and will signal you when remedial action is called for. This extends naturally to your business activities as well.

3. Pay attention if you find your thoughts are meandering or disconnected from your work priorities. Something is amiss.

4. If your business is failing, perhaps it is time to reflect on your next venture or life pathway.

5. Perhaps the best advice of all is to take a break and a step back to evaluate exactly what is going on, what might be impacting upon your entrepreneurial pathway, and what your options might be, either resolution or change. Reflect deeply before you act.

CHAPTER 18

We Are Only Human

Stories From the Trenches

Presentation Sabotage

I was invited to speak at a high-level investors conference in Tianjin, China. My role was to promote all the wonderful investment opportunities available in our region, from real estate and technology, to natural resources and tourism.

My PowerPoint was very carefully structured so that there were a number of "wow" pregnant pauses throughout that were intended to dazzle the audience and get them reaching for their checkbooks. With only 15 minutes to speak, the presentation was designed to capitalize on every second.

My assistant at the conference was this amazingly clever and gorgeous young Chinese woman whose main purpose, as I later found out, was to snare a Western capitalist and be swept away to the land of fashion and American decadence. She was an unintended distraction.

She dressed the part of the vamp in flimsy, semitransparent tops, spray on skirts, and six-inch stilettos. I had to have several discussions about this because I became worried that her focus was not on properly setting up my presentation and making me look good but on making herself flirtatiously irresistible to many of the other guest speakers. I think she resented my stifling her ambition.

When my speech delivery time arrived, I stepped up confidently to the podium and launched into my manicured PowerPoint, only to discover that the slide transition had been tampered with. New slides were flashing across the giant screen, nonstop, at the rate of a new slide every three seconds. It was impossible to fix the settings in the far-off media control room.

My presentation was an exercise in speed-talking. I probably sounded like a cattle auctioneer, and, while I salvaged what I could, I could not help notice my assistant sitting in the front row, exhibiting a slight "gotcha" smirk on her perfectly made up face.

And If I Were You...

1. Take nothing for granted, especially when you have a little bit of exposure time to make a big impression. Check everything that you are using to promote, and that includes demos, PowerPoints, handout materials ... everything.
2. At conferences and trade shows, do test runs of your presentations. Sometimes stuff gets lost in the transition as your material passes through numerous hands.
3. Where you are in need of a foreign-based host/hostess or translator, carry out interviews to make sure they are right for you and that they understand the goals of your visit.

What Do You *Want* Me to Say?

One aspect of my consulting business was packaging and marketing businesses for investment or divestiture. It was a bit of an artform, combining facts and promotion, and tailoring the presentations to the preferences and interests of the identified money players.

It worked more often than it did not. Most of our clients had the track record and market presence to make a good impression to outside parties. They also had excellent people, including the founders, who were versed in every aspect of their business and could field questions, even those thrown from left field.

In some instances, I was mandated to market and possibly license a technology for sale. The technology ranged from communications and health sciences to resource management. What made that type of sale tougher is that I had techies and scientists seated on both sides of the table. The buyers wanted to know as much proof-of-concept as they could, and the sellers were suspicious introverts with limited social skills.

In hindsight, this could have been an ideal training grounds for psychologists dealing with gawky children who were seemingly being compelled to share a sandbox.

On one occasion, I was in the midst of trying to sell an interesting piece of a highly complex land-based aquaculture process to the largest Asian seafood grower. My client's methodology included a mass of computer-controlled systems monitoring the health of the grow, including temperature controls, auto-feeders, antibiotic inflows, and, well, I think you get it. My Asian buyers, on the other hand, raised their product in trenches and threw in feed and chemicals by the shovel-full. The gap was enormous.

The buyers asked tons of questions, and the sellers grew increasingly suspicious and flustered, to the point that some of their answers conflicted with each other.

It was difficult to mediate this shifting scenario, but we were all managing, until the seller became progressively unhinged, turned to me, and in response to a buyers' question, said, "What do you want me to say? I can tell them anything you want me to. Do you want me to make something up?"

Credibility was instantly shot. The meeting broke up shortly afterward in total silence. I had never witnessed such a collapse before.

And If I Were You…

1. Prepare your team and your clients well, and do so beforehand.
2. Don't let your client improvise any responses.
3. Keep in mind that foreign business cultures may have different ethics and scruples. They are not necessarily playing by your rules.
4. Control the situation to the extent that the ground rules are clear to all parties.
5. One final tidbit of advice. When dealmaking, try to get a good-faith, nonreimbursable deposit from the interested party. Money tends to keep people a tad honest.

What the Heck Is That Smell?

My appointment was to meet the CEO of a large chicken processing plant. With over 200 employees and a sprawling factory in the countryside,

I was excited to try to add them to my client base. Their plan to expand the facility was exactly the kind of consulting contract I could readily undertake.

Arriving at the plant, the first thing I noticed was that the parking lot was 99% full. Finding the one, solitary spot to squeeze into seemed like a gift.

The meeting went extremely well, except for the fact that the CEO insisted on giving me a thorough tour of the plant. I mean, thorough. I am not one to complain about queasiness, but what these birds go through before they get to your table is humane but quite harsh. The "icing on the cake" was the last stage of production where the birds were eviscerated, and the fallout was collected and dried to make, you guessed it, chicken feed. Kind of like meeting your relatives over and over again.

I closed the deal, and quite happily, staggered out to the parking lot, only to notice the huge exhaust pipe suspended over my car. It was spewing the steam from the processing plant.

The result of that experience was threefold; (1) I signed a large consulting contract which, alas, also committed me to numerous visits back to the plant; (2) I swore off eating chicken for six months; and (3) I had to sell my car. I could not get rid of the pungent aroma that had belched into every corner of my car, even seeping through my window, which had been left open a tiny crack.

And If I Were You...

1. Do your homework before you meet clients. There is usually a ton of information available. It will better prepare you for what you may be walking into.

2. As you grow your business, you will have the opportunity to be selective in the clients you take on. If your business has grown beyond the "cash flow files," you take on more so to just pay the bills, then you have the option to walk away.

This brings to mind another time, after I had grown my company, when I was invited to bid on a lucrative contract for a development company that designed the software systems for warheads and missiles.

I politely declined. I was fortunately able to let my conscience guide my actions.

My Office Became a Dating/Hook-Up Service

As my consulting practice grew, I diligently searched for bright, young MBA graduates to constantly build up our team. They were mostly talented, entitled urban professionals eager to prove their worth and seemingly keen to negotiate salaries and perks as they had been taught to do in their MBA programs. Too true.

The team of nattily dressed and coiffed men and women grew, and I was increasingly proud of what I was building. They all received real-world training, including the art of dealing with authentic human beings (communications), a skill set that was apparently overlooked by academia.

As our projects portfolio grew, I organized weekly meetings to get updates from each of them as to progress and problems, but as the team grew, the meetings became "shallower." The degree of progress declined to the point of virtual stagnation, and I was determined to find out why.

I spent more time in the consultants' bullpen and lunch hour pub get-togethers, and to my utter surprise, I soon discovered that the mainstay of conversations between them was gossip; who was bedding who, who was rejected by who, who was "experimenting" with who, and so on. We had become a dating hookup service. Testosterone permeated the staff bullpen. While they played the field (and played, and played), my clients were becoming increasingly frustrated at the lack of focus and attention.

I put a stop to this by creating an Operations Manual, which included do's and don'ts. There was no behavior frowned upon as it was not up to me to judge, except that, on company time, personal relationships were to be suspended. It worked.

And If I Were You…

1. People are people. Human instincts generally prevail. As you start to employ people or grow your staff, assume there will be issues to deal with beyond the scope of your business practice.

2. Create an Operations Manual that highlights what is acceptable and what is not. Be clear on the consequences of your people's actions, obviously within the scope of human rights regulations and guidelines.

3. Carry out regular meetings with your people. This will highlight issues and give you the opportunity to demonstrate how wise you are as you offer direction and advice.

4. Set standards and milestones to be achieved for all, including a "division of responsibility" to identify who is responsible to whom when things unforeseen hit the fan, and they will.

Never Count on Anyone Who Has Nothing to Lose

I jumped at the opportunity to corner a mineral market and was diligently doing the equivalent of "land assembly" by tying up all known deposits and quarrying operations. Things were proceeding well, until I met Bob.

Bob was a dealmaker "extraordinaire," as he described himself. He would regale everyone with stories about his victories, with little empathy for the trail of "losers" he left behind. "After all," he would say, "they are just losers, and they are only good for making me money." He was ruthless, but I soldiered on.

My greed drove me onward. I needed Bob's industry connections and his clients' properties. I had him sign a Nondisclosure Agreement (NDA), which, as it turned out, was the last time I naively thought an NDA could protect me. Bob signed it very quickly without even reading it, which, in hindsight, should have been another red flag. It obviously meant nothing to him.

Let me describe Bob. At my very first meeting, he was on the phone with his Lamborghini dealership brutally berating them for selling someone else in town a Lamborghini the same model and color as his. Yet, even as I started cluing in to this rogue, my greed masked my apprehension in dealing with him.

In the end, after I had divulged my gameplan, and under the protection of an NDA, he did an end-run on me.

And If I Were You...

1. Listen to what businesspeople gossip about others. Horror stories have some truth to them.
2. Don't deal with crooks. You know pretty quickly who and what they are. Don't approach them. Don't trust them. Don't believe them.
3. Know that scruples and wealth are sometimes incompatible.
4. The obvious is often not the intended outcome. Think about what others may want out of a deal or transaction, and how it should alter your thinking and expectations, and your position in any client interaction.

Have You Ever Been Tarred and Feathered?

My assignment was to analyze the economic opportunities within a specific large region and make recommendations for some diversification that could offer employment and entrepreneurial possibilities to the resource-sector workforce about to be laid off.

They were a tough crowd. Generations employed at the lumber mill. Generous wages. Strong union. Outspoken leaders. In fact, the plant was already being dismantled and trucked away, and the workers were still picketing in what was obviously a comically futile measure.

I arrived, wallcharts and PowerPoints in hand, with a number of what I thought would be welcome ideas and opportunities to consider. In retrospect, I should have analyzed the population a lot better, with an understanding of what their expectations were, their history, and their level of contempt for the "suits."

I was deemed a "suit," an outsider. The ideas I had developed were very much "ivory tower arrogant" without me getting a better understanding and feel for what I was walking into.

My first suggestion was to develop nature tourism, high end eco-resorts and fly-in lodges. As soon as the word "eco" left my lips, I lost the audience. Grumblings about strangers invading their space and cowtowing to tourists did not sit well.

I moved onto my backup, sure-fire opportunity. Build a prison. This was an isolated and rural region. A prison offered over 300, well-paid jobs and a ton of job security. As well, there would be trickle-down/secondary industry development with support services, infrastructure, and more. I had already cleared the prospect with the government agency responsible, and they were on board.

It was at this point that several of the rowdier, roughneck unemployed workers actually started suggesting "tar and feather this guy." I had obviously outlived my welcome.

In the end, they voted to build a prison, and now have a healthy, stable economy around the facility, with direct and indirect employment at peak levels.

I never received an apology or a welcome back for the ribbon-cutting ceremony. However, every once in a while, I do have a nightmare about me, tarred and feathered and run out of town on a flatbed truck, with "Bubba's Towing" emblazoned on the door.

And If I Were You…

1. Know your audience. Do your homework before you meet a client. There are limitless sources to access information about anything or anybody.
2. Think "people." You are not dealing with businesses or government, but with the decision-making people impacting and being impacted by your ideas.
3. Avoid ivory tower thinking. It causes resentment at all levels.
4. Be genuine, sensitive, and sincerely involved in all your dealings. That makes friends, and those friends refer their friends, and so on.
5. Work hard to get client buy-in.
6. Know that, just because you make a suggestion, it doesn't necessarily mean you are right or that it will be well received. You may be good, even great at what you do, but you are likely playing in someone else's sandbox.

Demos That Bomb: What Then?

One of the very best ways to sell a business idea or company is by carrying out a demo right in front of the investors. Even if the demo is a crude mockup, there is an element of credibility seeing it work.

When I have technology or "gizmo" clients and my mandate is to search out and match up investment capital, I strive to get the client to construct a demo. It definitely adds some "wow" factor to any presentation.

In one particular instance, my client had developed a stock predictive model using artificial intelligence (AI). Each of the two founders had excellent credentials. One was a successful broker, and the other a university professor of AI Technology and Integration.

I watched their model work with "play money," and the gains were impressive. It was ready for an investor demo, or so I thought.

The investor meeting went exceptionally well. The money players, mostly successful stock market brokers, watched and salivated as the model bought and sold stock and churned out paper profits. The one question that was raised was "Has this model actually made any real investments and real profits?"

The answer was "no." This did not deter the prospective investors who pooled $25,000 for my client to invest, using their AI model, and report back in two weeks.

Apparently, and unbeknownst to me, the risk factors within the model were infinitely adjustable. The founders, now concerned about losing any real money, dumbed down the model to minimize risk. This also shifted the model from an AI model to a risk-adverse AD ("artificial dumb") model.

We returned to the investors' boardroom with a check of $1,086.75, which was the leftovers of their investment pool. It was an embarrassing learning experience.

And If I Were You…

1. Creating a "show me" demo is a great idea to win over investors. Just make sure the demo actually works.
2. Wherever feasible, have the founders put some of their own "skin on the table." In that way, they will be more cautious about making extravagant claims.
3. It is wise to also engage an arms-length third party to preview the product or technology being offered for investment or sale, and let them play the unrestrained "devil's advocate."

Never Do Business With Family or Friends

In designing and then building a non-nutritive cellulose fiber plant, I put key parcels out to bid with various contractors. One of those components was the intricate electrical system.

Because the plant needed to be explosion-proof, as well as being capable of sequentially starting over 5,000 horsepower of heavy equipment, the electrical requirement bid was carefully written to code, and went out as a fixed-cost contract proposal.

I have always been very suspicious of cost-plus contracts, and since we were on a reasonably strict four-million-dollar capital cost budget, only fixed-cost contracts would give us the budgetary control we needed.

My partner's brother was an industrial electrical contractor, and I was more than happy to have him included in the list of bidders. Most of the bids came in around $250,000 fixed, except for my partner's brother, which came in at cost plus 10 percent.

As you might imagine, arguments ensued, but in the end, I was assured by my partner and his brother that this was the most reasonable approach and we would be saving money as well. I conceded.

The electrical costs came in at $675,699. No explanations could satisfy me that I had not been duped. The partnership survived but was never quite the same.

And If I Were You...

1. Never do business with friends or family.
2. If you insist on doing business with friends or family, keep their "feet to the fire." Don't assume anyone is doing you any favors.
3. Finally, I am not sure I mentioned this, but don't do business with friends or family.

Think Long-Term Potential

My client was in the digital media sector. They had developed some very sophisticated software modeling, which, at the time, was quite revolutionary. The software could walk anybody through an object, such as an aircraft's internal workings or some hazardous facilities, and help identify design or problem issues. This was extremely leading edge.

The company was owned by a small handful of brilliant techies and media mavens who had deserted the film and early gaming industry to join forces on this venture. They were succeeding.

The problem was they did not have enough money to complete the technology and bring it to market. Their offices were located in a shabby, unheated warehouse. None of them drove a car newer than 10 years old. But they were a committed bunch, and I admired that all their resources went into the product development, and not into showy overheads.

I managed to find them some very keen investors who signed off on providing sufficient funding for the company to commercialize the product. Now came the important part—my fees.

I was offered payment in line with my consulting contract, or, alternatively, shares representing a 5 percent stake in the business. I opted for payment, likely because my company was also in its infancy and my long-term thinking represented meeting payroll and rent.

As the years progressed, I read about the company getting involved in major motion picture 3D graphics in such films as *The Abyss*, *Terminator*, and *Jurassic Park*. I was most pleased to have been part of their road to success.

Then one day, the company's founder had his photo adorning the business section of a national magazine, announcing that they had just been acquired by Lucasfilm for a veritable fortune.

I was still very pleased for them but far less proud about my short-term thinking.

And If I Were You...

1. Business often presents opportunities like no other venue can. But these flashes are brief, and fleeting. Don't let them escape before you think long and hard about what is on the table.
2. Business often comes down to acting on your gut feel. That is fine, but don't let greed blindside your judgment.

3. Sometimes, you need to take a flyer. If it doesn't damage or impair your business, or shift focus away from your business plan and gameplan, then maybe go for it.

4. New opportunities are often blindingly exciting. The opposite is wearing horse blinders and seeing nothing other than what lies straight ahead. Success in business is achieved somewhere in between.

Bribery Should Have Worked

I once got involved in a wild negotiation to buy a patent. I was concerned that this patent might step on the one that I already owned, and I wanted to take them out of the game.

Negotiations got off to a great start as we all agreed that the patent owner wanted to sell, and that I wanted to buy. All we had to do was work out the terms of the deal.

The patent owner was a great guy and we got along well right from the first hello. He wasn't very savvy in working out deal terms, so he had hired a local lawyer to help him. His lawyer was, well, a lawyer, and more interested in creating and adding so much complexity to this deal that it became undoable. After an unproductive day of negotiating, nothing had really progressed. He still wanted to sell and I still wanted to buy, but the deal-wrecking lawyer was in our way.

In a classic case of "know your customer," I retrenched and found a better way to get this purchase done. During our "*get to know you*" conversations, I learned that the patent owner was a long-haul truck driver. Pay dirt! That night, I researched the long-haul truck models and picked out a deluxe one to buy for him, to entice him into the deal. In the morning, I contacted a local truck dealer and agreed on a model and price.

Day two negotiations started off with me presenting him with a brochure of his expensive soon-to-arrive new truck. The deal was that he gets his dream truck, and I get the patent. Smiles all around. Life should be that easy.

In the end, the lawyer reinstated himself into the deal and the whole thing blew up. He didn't get his truck and I didn't get the patent. Nobody was happy, but I guess the lawyer got paid.

Don't ever let a lawyer near deal making.

And If I Were You...

1. Be prepared to change gears during any negotiation as long as you get what you need.
2. I love lawyers, but don't ever involve them in deal making. Lawyers should paper deals, not make deals. They should be following your instructions to legalize what the parties themselves had agreed upon.

Getting Pressured Into Hiring the Brain-Dead

I was once maneuvered into hiring the boss's friend. In this case, the boss was actually one of my key investors who had subtly requested that I "consider" hiring his side kick. His suggestion didn't leave me much maneuvering room, and I reluctantly hired him.

The side kick was a gregarious, outgoing guy who we tasked with a number of special projects for the company. He achieved a mixed bag of minor successes. However, each time he failed, he simply ran back and bad mouthed the company to his friend, the investor. It was always the company's fault and never his.

His constant and vindictive stream of complaints to our investor was destabilizing the relationship with the investor and undermining the company's expansion plans. He needed to be stopped, without damaging my rapport with the investor.

My strategy was to assign him to work on increasing complex issues where he was in way over his head. This assured his ongoing string of failures. I had been maneuvered into hiring him, and now I was maneuvering to get rid of him.

It didn't take much time for him to become totally disheartened. His next conversation with our investor was to advise him that he was going to leave the company and, most importantly, that it was his decision.

I had mixed feelings about the outcome. On the one hand, I had spent too much time and energy on this distraction. But, by setting him up to fail, I successfully got rid of the nuisance without devastating my relationship with a key investor. As ugly as this experience was, I chalked it up as a win.

And If I Were You...

1. Hiring someone because they are the boss's friend will never end well.
2. Always control the communications lines between your company and its investors.

Always Avoid Murder Suspects

When you travel extensively, constantly creating relationships and setting up deals, you meet a lot of interesting people. This was certainly the case when I was setting up operations for a company in California.

Upon arriving in LA, I hit the ground running. I met with several companies that would be ideal showcase customers, and one company jumped out immediately. Their owner was keen to help us launch, and he turned out to be the local *fixer* that we needed. He smoothed the way through the regulatory process, gave us a physical presence in California, and coordinated our efforts at his company. He was also very highly thought of in his industry. I was thrilled.

Our roll-out was flawless, right up to the day that our *fixer* got arrested. This wasn't just a case of jaywalking or spiting in public. He was charged as an accessory in a gang murder that involved illegal guns and drugs. He subsequently pleaded guilty and was shipped off to prison for a long visit.

I deleted him from my speed dial as fast as I could, and I suspect that a lot of other people did too. His name was never mentioned again in the industry.

You always joke about the person that you're working closely with as your "partner in crime." I never used this expression again.

And If I Were You...

1. Avoid doing business with murder suspects seems like some good advice to pass along. Yes, you're welcome.
2. Laugh and learn from your mistakes. There is always another hiccup lurking out there.

About the Authors

Jay J. Silverberg is a "business rebel" who has started and run a number of successful businesses. This book is a culmination of his business adventures (and misadventures) and offers up a multitude of inestimably valuable lessons. As an entrepreneurial trainer, Jay has developed innovative programs for both the beginner and the advanced businessperson, and delivered training and mentoring to thousands of entrepreneurs, managers, and business professionals.

As a business consultant, Jay's practice ranges from startups to Fortune 500 firms with projects that have spanned the globe. He has also represented government, trade, and economic development ministries at the national and international conferences.

Jay Silverberg currently teaches various levels of entrepreneurship and delivers business coaching and mentoring.

Jay resides in Vancouver, British Columbia, Canada with his wife, Linda, who inspires him to always see life as a gift, and business as a game (and vice versa). Jay can be contacted at silverberg88@gmail.com.

Related Books

Silverberg, J.J. October 2020. *A Business Cynic's Wisdom: Winning Through Flexible Ethics*, Business Expert Press.

Bruce E. McLean is a business veteran who has extensive experience with startups and high-growth companies. He has designed and delivered sales and operations programs throughout the United States and Canada.

Bruce's expertise led him to dealings with major companies in some of North America's toughest boardrooms. In his diverse business activities, Bruce has pioneered advertising and technology companies and set up a manufacturing presence in China.

Regardless of all his big picture experience, Bruce is a dedicated startup junkie and can't resist jumping in to help launch the next "big thing." He was part of small team that grew a one office startup into a 500 employee company. As he is fond of saying, "you don't have to break the rules, you just make new ones."

His business adventures span national and international marketplaces. Bruce's exploits add entertaining and lesson-worthy escapades throughout this book.

Bruce is an avid sports fan and never misses a Seahawks game—*Go Hawks*! He can be contacted at bmclean.langley@gmail.com.

Both authors have an abundance of real-world business "stories" that translate into critical business advice for business students, executives, and both new and established entrepreneurs.

Index

OTHER TITLES IN THE ENTREPRENEURSHIP AND SMALL BUSINESS MANAGEMENT COLLECTION

Scott Shane, Case Western University, Editor

- *The 8 Superpowers of Successful Entrepreneurs* by Marina Nicholas
- *Founders, Freelancers & Rebels* by Helen Jane Campbell
- *Time Management for Unicorns* by Giulio D'Agostino
- *Zero to $10 Million* by Shane Brett
- *Navigating the New Normal* by Rodd Mann
- *Ethical Business Culture* by Andreas Karaoulanis
- *Blockchain Value* by Olga V. Mack
- *TAP Into Your Potential* by Rick De La Guardia
- *Stop, Change, Grow* by Michael Carter and Karl Shaikh
- *Dynastic Planning* by Walid S. Chiniara
- *From Starting Small to Winning Big* by Shishir Mishra
- *How to Succeed as a Solo Consultant* by Stephen D. Field
- *Native American Entrepreneurs* by Ron P. Sheffield and J. Mark Munoz
- *The Entrepreneurial Adventure* by David James and Oliver James

Concise and Applied Business Books

The Collection listed above is one of 30 business subject collections that Business Expert Press has grown to make BEP a premiere publisher of print and digital books. Our concise and applied books are for...

- Professionals and Practitioners
- Faculty who adopt our books for courses
- Librarians who know that BEP's Digital Libraries are a unique way to offer students ebooks to download, not restricted with any digital rights management
- Executive Training Course Leaders
- Business Seminar Organizers

Business Expert Press books are for anyone who needs to dig deeper on business ideas, goals, and solutions to everyday problems. Whether one print book, one ebook, or buying a digital library of 110 ebooks, we remain the affordable and smart way to be business smart. For more information, please visit www.businessexpertpress.com, or contact sales@businessexpertpress.com.